Notes

NurseThink™ Notes
Note Taking That Works!

Tim Bristol, PhD, RN, CNE, ANEF
Faculty - Walden University
Minneapolis, Minnesota

Karin J. Sherrill, MSN, RN, CNE, ANEF
Faculty - Maricopa Community Colleges
Phoenix, Arizona

NurseThink.com
NurseThink.com/adopt
NurseThink.com/samples

NurseTim.com • 866.861.2896

Published by NurseTim, Inc., P.O. Box 86, Waconia, MN 55387

No part of this publication may be reproduced, stored in a retrieval system, or transmitted in any form or by any means, electronic, mechanical, photocopying, recording, scanning, or otherwise, except as permitted under Section 107 or 108 of the 1976 United States Copyright Act, without either the prior written permission of the publisher. Requests to publisher for permission should be addressed to the Permission Department, NurseTim, Inc., P.O. Box 86, Waconia, MN 55387, 866.861.2896, fax 866.861.2896, or online at www.NurseTim.com.

Additional copies of this publication are available at www.NurseThink.com

Limit of Liability/Disclaimer of Warranty: While the publisher and author have used their best efforts in preparing this book, they make no representations or warranties with respect to the accuracy or completeness of the contents of this book and specifically disclaim any implied warranties of merchantability or fitness for a particular purpose.

ISBN 978-0-692-78988-9

Printed in the United States of America
Second Edition
0 9 8 7 6 5 4 3 2 1

NCLEX® is a registered trademark for the National Council of State Boards of Nursing, Inc.

Learning how to learn is essential to every nursing student. Because there is no way to know every fact, a clear and consistent process for managing information will help students develop deep understanding that will cross all clinical situations. NurseThink Notes puts that process in an easy-to-manage tool. This unique tool is ideal for class, reading, studying, collaboration, and even clinical preparation.

As students begin using NurseThink Notes, they will use critical-thinking skills to prioritize information essential to obtain desired outcomes. Through a carefully- designed process of application and analysis, long-term retention and, more importantly, the ability to adjust to a variety of situations will be facilitated.

Finally, NurseThink Notes saves students and faculty time. When concepts can be clearly organized and easily accessed, students will have better outcomes. Students and faculty can do a better job of communicating about concepts (referencing key sections and analyzing the overall layout of the material). Time saving is important, as we want students more engaged in applying the information to patient care (case studies, simulations, clinical experiences, etc.) and less time involved in "acquiring" the knowledge.

STUDENT TIPS FOR SUCCESS

Best practice study tips
- While completing your reading, homework, and classroom activities, you will be organizing information in *NurseThink Notes*.
- Attend and actively engage in class. The classroom facilitator will offer some direction as to where to focus your study. After class (within 24 hours for best success) summarize your classroom discussions on your *NurseThink Notes*.
- Remember you only can choose 3 priorities in each area, so select wisely.

Strategies for prioritizing care
- Airway, breathing, circulation.
- Maslow hierarchy; physiologic needs first.
- Determine which findings/potential complications will lead to the greatest chance of mortality or morbidity.
- Identify least invasive interventions first
- Always consider safety.
- Use the nursing process to identify priorities (assessment, diagnosis, planning, implementation, evaluation)
- Encourage and support self-care with your patient

Care According to the NCLEX® Test Plan
These categories are the emphasized areas of your licensure exam. It is important that you become familiar with them so you can best prepare. To see the details of each category, explore the Test Blueprint for the licensure exam you will be taking. (www.ncsbn.org)

Quality and Safety Standards
National care and safety standards guide our practice. Becoming familiar and applying each of these standards will best prepare you for practice. Consider the situation for your patient with each condition, what emphasis needs to be placed in providing quality and safety.

NurseThink Notes tutorials and additional resources are available at www.NurseThink.com

CONTENTS

= High Frequency Patient Alerts from AARP, AHRQ, CDC and Healthy People 2020   = NurseThink Quick!

⎍ = High Frequency Patient Alerts from AARP, AHRQ, CDC and Healthy People 2020   ⚡ = NurseThink Quick!

Related Exemplars	**Related Concepts**

Classroom Critical Thinking	**Reading / Resources Critical Thinking**

Priority Assessments	**Priority Labs & Diagnostics**	**Priority Nursing Interventions**
1	1	1
2	2	2
3	3	3

Priority Medications	**Priority Potential & Actual Complications**	**Priority Collaborative Goals**
1	1	1
2	2	2
3	3	3

NurseThink Quick

<table>
<tr><td></td><td></td><td></td></tr>
</table>

CARE ACCORDING TO THE NCLEX® TEST PLAN

Safe and Effective Care: Management of Care, Coordinated Care, Safety and Infection Control

Health Promotion and Maintenance

Psychosocial Integrity

Physiological Integrity: Basic Care and Comfort, Pharmacological and Parenteral Therapies, Reduction of Risk Potential, and Physiological Adaptation

CARE ACCORDING TO QUALITY AND SAFETY STANDARDS

Patient-Centered Care

Teamwork and Collaboration

Evidence-Based Practice

Quality Improvement

Safety

Informatics

Buddy Review: _____   Faculty Review: _____

Grade Tracker

<table>
<tr><td></td><td></td><td></td><td></td><td></td><td></td><td></td><td></td><td></td><td></td><td></td><td></td><td></td><td></td><td></td><td></td></tr>
</table>

Related Exemplars	Related Concepts

Classroom Critical Thinking	Reading / Resources Critical Thinking

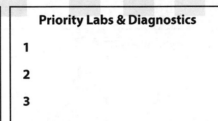

Priority Assessments	Priority Labs & Diagnostics	Priority Nursing Interventions
1	1	1
2	2	2
3	3	3

Priority Medications	Priority Potential & Actual Complications	Priority Collaborative Goals
1	1	1
2	2	2
3	3	3

NurseThink Quick

CARE ACCORDING TO THE NCLEX® TEST PLAN

Safe and Effective Care: Management of Care, Coordinated Care, Safety and Infection Control

Health Promotion and Maintenance

Psychosocial Integrity

Physiological Integrity: Basic Care and Comfort, Pharmacological and Parenteral Therapies, Reduction of Risk Potential, and Physiological Adaptation

CARE ACCORDING TO QUALITY AND SAFETY STANDARDS

Patient-Centered Care

Teamwork and Collaboration

Evidence-Based Practice

Quality Improvement

Safety

Informatics

Buddy Review: _____   Faculty Review: _____

Grade Tracker

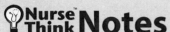

Related Exemplars	**Related Concepts**

Classroom Critical Thinking	**Reading / Resources Critical Thinking**

Priority Assessments

1
2
3

Priority Labs & Diagnostics

1
2
3

Priority Nursing Interventions

1
2
3

Priority Medications

1

2

3

Priority Potential & Actual Complications

1

2

3

Priority Collaborative Goals

1

2

3

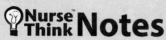
NurseThink Quick

CARE ACCORDING TO THE NCLEX® TEST PLAN

Safe and Effective Care: Management of Care, Coordinated Care, Safety and Infection Control

Health Promotion and Maintenance

Psychosocial Integrity

Physiological Integrity: Basic Care and Comfort, Pharmacological and Parenteral Therapies, Reduction of Risk Potential, and Physiological Adaptation

CARE ACCORDING TO QUALITY AND SAFETY STANDARDS

Patient-Centered Care

Teamwork and Collaboration

Evidence-Based Practice

Quality Improvement

Safety

Informatics

Buddy Review: _____   Faculty Review: _____

Grade Tracker

Related Exemplars	Related Concepts

Classroom Critical Thinking	Reading / Resources Critical Thinking

Priority Assessments	Priority Labs & Diagnostics	Priority Nursing Interventions
1	1	1
2	2	2
3	3	3

Priority Medications	Priority Potential & Actual Complications	Priority Collaborative Goals
1	1	1
2	2	2
3	3	3

NurseThink Quick

CARE ACCORDING TO THE NCLEX® TEST PLAN

Safe and Effective Care: Management of Care, Coordinated Care, Safety and Infection Control

Health Promotion and Maintenance

Psychosocial Integrity

Physiological Integrity: Basic Care and Comfort, Pharmacological and Parenteral Therapies, Reduction of Risk Potential, and Physiological Adaptation

CARE ACCORDING TO QUALITY AND SAFETY STANDARDS

Patient-Centered Care

Teamwork and Collaboration

Evidence-Based Practice

Quality Improvement

Safety

Informatics

Buddy Review: _____   Faculty Review: _____

Grade Tracker

Related Exemplars

Related Concepts

Classroom Critical Thinking

Reading / Resources Critical Thinking

Priority Assessments

1

2

3

Priority Labs & Diagnostics

1

2

3

Priority Nursing Interventions

1

2

3

Priority Medications

1

2

3

Priority Potential & Actual Complications

1

2

3

Priority Collaborative Goals

1

2

3

NurseThink Quick

CARE ACCORDING TO THE NCLEX® TEST PLAN

Safe and Effective Care: Management of Care, Coordinated Care, Safety and Infection Control

Health Promotion and Maintenance

Psychosocial Integrity

Physiological Integrity: Basic Care and Comfort, Pharmacological and Parenteral Therapies, Reduction of Risk Potential, and Physiological Adaptation

CARE ACCORDING TO QUALITY AND SAFETY STANDARDS

Patient-Centered Care

Teamwork and Collaboration

Evidence-Based Practice

Quality Improvement

Safety

Informatics

Buddy Review: _____   Faculty Review: _____

Grade Tracker

 **Notes**

Related Exemplars

Related Concepts

Classroom Critical Thinking

Reading / Resources Critical Thinking

Priority Assessments
1
2
3

Priority Labs & Diagnostics
1
2
3

Priority Nursing Interventions
1
2
3

Priority Medications
1
2
3

Priority Potential & Actual Complications
1
2
3

Priority Collaborative Goals
1
2
3

NurseThink Quick

<table>
<tr><td></td><td></td><td></td></tr>
</table>

CARE ACCORDING TO THE NCLEX® TEST PLAN

Safe and Effective Care: Management of Care, Coordinated Care, Safety and Infection Control

Health Promotion and Maintenance

Psychosocial Integrity

Physiological Integrity: Basic Care and Comfort, Pharmacological and Parenteral Therapies, Reduction of Risk Potential, and Physiological Adaptation

CARE ACCORDING TO QUALITY AND SAFETY STANDARDS

Patient-Centered Care

Teamwork and Collaboration

Evidence-Based Practice

Quality Improvement

Safety

Informatics

Buddy Review: _____   Faculty Review: _____

Grade Tracker

<table>
<tr><td></td><td></td><td></td><td></td><td></td><td></td><td></td><td></td><td></td><td></td><td></td><td></td><td></td><td></td><td></td><td></td><td></td><td></td></tr>
</table>

Related Exemplars

Related Concepts

Classroom Critical Thinking

Reading / Resources Critical Thinking

Priority Assessments

1

2

3

Priority Labs & Diagnostics

1

2

3

Priority Nursing Interventions

1

2

3

Priority Medications

1

2

3

Priority Potential & Actual Complications

1

2

3

Priority Collaborative Goals

1

2

3

NurseThink Quick

<table>
<tr><td></td><td></td><td></td></tr>
</table>

CARE ACCORDING TO THE NCLEX® TEST PLAN

Safe and Effective Care: Management of Care, Coordinated Care, Safety and Infection Control

Health Promotion and Maintenance

Psychosocial Integrity

Physiological Integrity: Basic Care and Comfort, Pharmacological and Parenteral Therapies, Reduction of Risk Potential, and Physiological Adaptation

CARE ACCORDING TO QUALITY AND SAFETY STANDARDS

Patient-Centered Care

Teamwork and Collaboration

Evidence-Based Practice

Quality Improvement

Safety

Informatics

Buddy Review: _____   Faculty Review: _____

Grade Tracker

<table>
<tr><td></td><td></td><td></td><td></td><td></td><td></td><td></td><td></td><td></td><td></td><td></td><td></td><td></td><td></td><td></td><td></td></tr>
</table>

Related Exemplars	Related Concepts

Classroom Critical Thinking	Reading / Resources Critical Thinking

Priority Assessments	Priority Labs & Diagnostics	Priority Nursing Interventions
1	1	1
2	2	2
3	3	3

Priority Medications	Priority Potential & Actual Complications	Priority Collaborative Goals
1	1	1
2	2	2
3	3	3

NurseThink Notes

NurseThink Quick

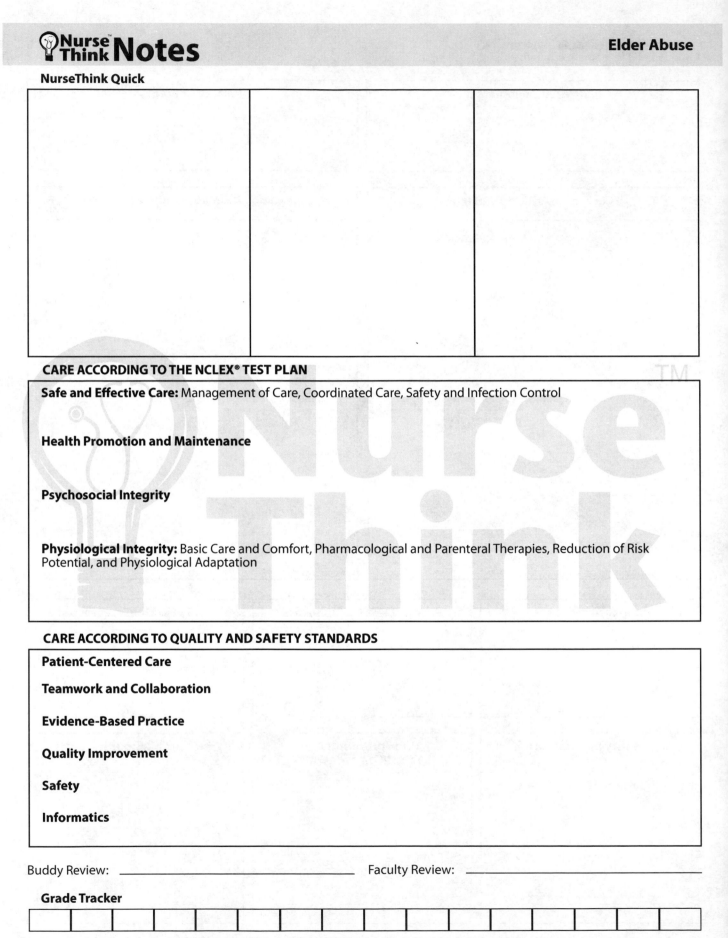

CARE ACCORDING TO THE NCLEX® TEST PLAN

Safe and Effective Care: Management of Care, Coordinated Care, Safety and Infection Control

Health Promotion and Maintenance

Psychosocial Integrity

Physiological Integrity: Basic Care and Comfort, Pharmacological and Parenteral Therapies, Reduction of Risk Potential, and Physiological Adaptation

CARE ACCORDING TO QUALITY AND SAFETY STANDARDS

Patient-Centered Care

Teamwork and Collaboration

Evidence-Based Practice

Quality Improvement

Safety

Informatics

Buddy Review: _____   Faculty Review: _____

Grade Tracker

Related Exemplars	Related Concepts

Classroom Critical Thinking	Reading / Resources Critical Thinking

Priority Assessments	Priority Labs & Diagnostics	Priority Nursing Interventions
1	1	1
2	2	2
3	3	3

Priority Medications	Priority Potential & Actual Complications	Priority Collaborative Goals
1	1	1
2	2	2
3	3	3

NurseThink Quick

CARE ACCORDING TO THE NCLEX® TEST PLAN

Safe and Effective Care: Management of Care, Coordinated Care, Safety and Infection Control

Health Promotion and Maintenance

Psychosocial Integrity

Physiological Integrity: Basic Care and Comfort, Pharmacological and Parenteral Therapies, Reduction of Risk Potential, and Physiological Adaptation

CARE ACCORDING TO QUALITY AND SAFETY STANDARDS

Patient-Centered Care

Teamwork and Collaboration

Evidence-Based Practice

Quality Improvement

Safety

Informatics

Buddy Review: _____   Faculty Review: _____

Grade Tracker

Related Exemplars

Related Concepts

Classroom Critical Thinking

Reading / Resources Critical Thinking

Priority Assessments

1

2

3

Priority Labs & Diagnostics

1

2

3

Priority Nursing Interventions

1

2

3

Priority Medications

1

2

3

Priority Potential & Actual Complications

1

2

3

Priority Collaborative Goals

1

2

3

NurseThink Quick

CARE ACCORDING TO THE NCLEX® TEST PLAN

Safe and Effective Care: Management of Care, Coordinated Care, Safety and Infection Control

Health Promotion and Maintenance

Psychosocial Integrity

Physiological Integrity: Basic Care and Comfort, Pharmacological and Parenteral Therapies, Reduction of Risk Potential, and Physiological Adaptation

CARE ACCORDING TO QUALITY AND SAFETY STANDARDS

Patient-Centered Care

Teamwork and Collaboration

Evidence-Based Practice

Quality Improvement

Safety

Informatics

Buddy Review: _____   Faculty Review: _____

Grade Tracker

Related Exemplars	**Related Concepts**

Classroom Critical Thinking	**Reading / Resources Critical Thinking**

Priority Assessments

1
2
3

Priority Labs & Diagnostics

1
2
3

Priority Nursing Interventions

1
2
3

Priority Medications

1
2
3

Priority Potential & Actual Complications

1
2
3

Priority Collaborative Goals

1
2
3

NurseThink Quick

CARE ACCORDING TO THE NCLEX® TEST PLAN

Safe and Effective Care: Management of Care, Coordinated Care, Safety and Infection Control

Health Promotion and Maintenance

Psychosocial Integrity

Physiological Integrity: Basic Care and Comfort, Pharmacological and Parenteral Therapies, Reduction of Risk Potential, and Physiological Adaptation

CARE ACCORDING TO QUALITY AND SAFETY STANDARDS

Patient-Centered Care

Teamwork and Collaboration

Evidence-Based Practice

Quality Improvement

Safety

Informatics

Buddy Review: _____   Faculty Review: _____

Grade Tracker

Related Exemplars	**Related Concepts**

Classroom Critical Thinking	**Reading / Resources Critical Thinking**

Priority Assessments

1

2

3

Priority Labs & Diagnostics

1

2

3

Priority Nursing Interventions

1

2

3

Priority Medications

1

2

3

Priority Potential & Actual Complications

1

2

3

Priority Collaborative Goals

1

2

3

NurseThink Quick

CARE ACCORDING TO THE NCLEX® TEST PLAN

Safe and Effective Care: Management of Care, Coordinated Care, Safety and Infection Control

Health Promotion and Maintenance

Psychosocial Integrity

Physiological Integrity: Basic Care and Comfort, Pharmacological and Parenteral Therapies, Reduction of Risk Potential, and Physiological Adaptation

CARE ACCORDING TO QUALITY AND SAFETY STANDARDS

Patient-Centered Care

Teamwork and Collaboration

Evidence-Based Practice

Quality Improvement

Safety

Informatics

Buddy Review: _____   Faculty Review: _____

Grade Tracker

Related Exemplars	Related Concepts

Classroom Critical Thinking	Reading / Resources Critical Thinking

Priority Assessments

1
2
3

Priority Labs & Diagnostics

1
2
3

Priority Nursing Interventions

1
2
3

Priority Medications

1
2
3

Priority Potential & Actual Complications

1
2
3

Priority Collaborative Goals

1
2
3

NurseThink Notes

NurseThink Quick

CARE ACCORDING TO THE NCLEX® TEST PLAN

Safe and Effective Care: Management of Care, Coordinated Care, Safety and Infection Control

Health Promotion and Maintenance

Psychosocial Integrity

Physiological Integrity: Basic Care and Comfort, Pharmacological and Parenteral Therapies, Reduction of Risk Potential, and Physiological Adaptation

CARE ACCORDING TO QUALITY AND SAFETY STANDARDS

Patient-Centered Care

Teamwork and Collaboration

Evidence-Based Practice

Quality Improvement

Safety

Informatics

Buddy Review: _____   Faculty Review: _____

Grade Tracker

 **Notes**

Related Exemplars

Related Concepts

Classroom Critical Thinking

Reading / Resources Critical Thinking

Priority Assessments
1
2
3

Priority Labs & Diagnostics
1
2
3

Priority Nursing Interventions
1
2
3

Priority Medications
1
2
3

Priority Potential & Actual Complications
1
2
3

Priority Collaborative Goals
1
2
3

NurseThink Quick

CARE ACCORDING TO THE NCLEX® TEST PLAN

Safe and Effective Care: Management of Care, Coordinated Care, Safety and Infection Control

Health Promotion and Maintenance

Psychosocial Integrity

Physiological Integrity: Basic Care and Comfort, Pharmacological and Parenteral Therapies, Reduction of Risk Potential, and Physiological Adaptation

CARE ACCORDING TO QUALITY AND SAFETY STANDARDS

Patient-Centered Care

Teamwork and Collaboration

Evidence-Based Practice

Quality Improvement

Safety

Informatics

Buddy Review: _____   Faculty Review: _____

Grade Tracker

Related Exemplars	Related Concepts

Classroom Critical Thinking	Reading / Resources Critical Thinking

Priority Assessments

1
2
3

Priority Labs & Diagnostics

1
2
3

Priority Nursing Interventions

1
2
3

Priority Medications

1

2

3

Priority Potential & Actual Complications

1

2

3

Priority Collaborative Goals

1

2

3

NurseThink Quick

Nicotinic Effects
MTWThF
Mydriasis/Muscle cramps
Tachycardia
Weakness
Twitching
Hypertension/Hyperglycemia
Fasciculation

CARE ACCORDING TO THE NCLEX® TEST PLAN

Safe and Effective Care: Management of Care, Coordinated Care, Safety and Infection Control

Health Promotion and Maintenance

Psychosocial Integrity

Physiological Integrity: Basic Care and Comfort, Pharmacological and Parenteral Therapies, Reduction of Risk Potential, and Physiological Adaptation

CARE ACCORDING TO QUALITY AND SAFETY STANDARDS

Patient-Centered Care

Teamwork and Collaboration

Evidence-Based Practice

Quality Improvement

Safety

Informatics

Buddy Review: _____   Faculty Review: _____

Grade Tracker

Related Exemplars	Related Concepts

Classroom Critical Thinking	Reading / Resources Critical Thinking

Priority Assessments	Priority Labs & Diagnostics	Priority Nursing Interventions
1	1	1
2	2	2
3	3	3

Priority Medications	Priority Potential & Actual Complications	Priority Collaborative Goals
1	1	1
2	2	2
3	3	3

NurseThink Quick

CARE ACCORDING TO THE NCLEX® TEST PLAN

Safe and Effective Care: Management of Care, Coordinated Care, Safety and Infection Control

Health Promotion and Maintenance

Psychosocial Integrity

Physiological Integrity: Basic Care and Comfort, Pharmacological and Parenteral Therapies, Reduction of Risk Potential, and Physiological Adaptation

CARE ACCORDING TO QUALITY AND SAFETY STANDARDS

Patient-Centered Care

Teamwork and Collaboration

Evidence-Based Practice

Quality Improvement

Safety

Informatics

Buddy Review: _____   Faculty Review: _____

Grade Tracker

Related Exemplars

Related Concepts

Classroom Critical Thinking

Reading / Resources Critical Thinking

Priority Assessments

1

2

3

Priority Labs & Diagnostics

1

2

3

Priority Nursing Interventions

1

2

3

Priority Medications

1

2

3

Priority Potential & Actual Complications

1

2

3

Priority Collaborative Goals

1

2

3

NurseThink Quick

CARE ACCORDING TO THE NCLEX® TEST PLAN

Safe and Effective Care: Management of Care, Coordinated Care, Safety and Infection Control

Health Promotion and Maintenance

Psychosocial Integrity

Physiological Integrity: Basic Care and Comfort, Pharmacological and Parenteral Therapies, Reduction of Risk Potential, and Physiological Adaptation

CARE ACCORDING TO QUALITY AND SAFETY STANDARDS

Patient-Centered Care

Teamwork and Collaboration

Evidence-Based Practice

Quality Improvement

Safety

Informatics

Buddy Review: _____   Faculty Review: _____

Grade Tracker

Related Exemplars

Related Concepts

Classroom Critical Thinking

Reading / Resources Critical Thinking

Priority Assessments

1
2
3

Priority Labs & Diagnostics

1
2
3

Priority Nursing Interventions

1
2
3

Priority Medications

1
2
3

Priority Potential & Actual Complications

1
2
3

Priority Collaborative Goals

1
2
3

NurseThink Quick

Abdominal Aortic Aneurism: Symptoms *4A's* **A**symptomatic **A**bdominal mass **A**bdominal pulse **A**ches in low back		

CARE ACCORDING TO THE NCLEX® TEST PLAN

Safe and Effective Care: Management of Care, Coordinated Care, Safety and Infection Control

Health Promotion and Maintenance

Psychosocial Integrity

Physiological Integrity: Basic Care and Comfort, Pharmacological and Parenteral Therapies, Reduction of Risk Potential, and Physiological Adaptation

CARE ACCORDING TO QUALITY AND SAFETY STANDARDS

Patient-Centered Care

Teamwork and Collaboration

Evidence-Based Practice

Quality Improvement

Safety

Informatics

Buddy Review: _____   Faculty Review: _____

Grade Tracker

Related Exemplars

Related Concepts

Classroom Critical Thinking

Reading / Resources Critical Thinking

Priority Assessments

1

2

3

Priority Labs & Diagnostics

1

2

3

Priority Nursing Interventions

1

2

3

Priority Medications

1

2

3

**Priority Potential &
Actual Complications**

1

2

3

Priority Collaborative Goals

1

2

3

NurseThink Notes

NurseThink Quick

CARE ACCORDING TO THE NCLEX® TEST PLAN

Safe and Effective Care: Management of Care, Coordinated Care, Safety and Infection Control

Health Promotion and Maintenance

Psychosocial Integrity

Physiological Integrity: Basic Care and Comfort, Pharmacological and Parenteral Therapies, Reduction of Risk Potential, and Physiological Adaptation

CARE ACCORDING TO QUALITY AND SAFETY STANDARDS

Patient-Centered Care

Teamwork and Collaboration

Evidence-Based Practice

Quality Improvement

Safety

Informatics

Buddy Review: _____   Faculty Review: _____

Grade Tracker

Related Exemplars	Related Concepts

Classroom Critical Thinking	Reading / Resources Critical Thinking

Priority Assessments

1

2

3

Priority Labs & Diagnostics

1

2

3

Priority Nursing Interventions

1

2

3

Priority Medications

1

2

3

Priority Potential & Actual Complications

1

2

3

Priority Collaborative Goals

1

2

3

NurseThink Quick

Raynaud's Phenomenon: Causes	Buerger's Disease Features	
Cold Hand	***Scraps***	
Cryoglobulins/Cryofibrinogens	**S**egmenting thrombosing vasculitis	
Obstruction/Occupational	**C**laudication	
Lupus	**R**aynaud's phenomenon	
Diabetes mellitus/Drugs	**A**ssociated with smoking	
Hematologic problems (polycythemia, leukemia)	**P**ain, even at rest	
Arterial problems (atherosclerosis)	**S**uperficial nodular phlebitis	
Neurologic problems (vascular tone)		
Disease of unknown origin (idiopathic)		

CARE ACCORDING TO THE NCLEX® TEST PLAN

Safe and Effective Care: Management of Care, Coordinated Care, Safety and Infection Control

Health Promotion and Maintenance

Psychosocial Integrity

Physiological Integrity: Basic Care and Comfort, Pharmacological and Parenteral Therapies, Reduction of Risk Potential, and Physiological Adaptation

CARE ACCORDING TO QUALITY AND SAFETY STANDARDS

Patient-Centered Care

Teamwork and Collaboration

Evidence-Based Practice

Quality Improvement

Safety

Informatics

Buddy Review: _____   Faculty Review: _____

Grade Tracker

Related Exemplars	**Related Concepts**

Classroom Critical Thinking	**Reading / Resources Critical Thinking**

Priority Assessments

1
2
3

Priority Labs & Diagnostics

1
2
3

Priority Nursing Interventions

1
2
3

Priority Medications

1
2
3

Priority Potential & Actual Complications

1
2
3

Priority Collaborative Goals

1
2
3

NurseThink Quick

CARE ACCORDING TO THE NCLEX® TEST PLAN

Safe and Effective Care: Management of Care, Coordinated Care, Safety and Infection Control

Health Promotion and Maintenance

Psychosocial Integrity

Physiological Integrity: Basic Care and Comfort, Pharmacological and Parenteral Therapies, Reduction of Risk Potential, and Physiological Adaptation

CARE ACCORDING TO QUALITY AND SAFETY STANDARDS

Patient-Centered Care

Teamwork and Collaboration

Evidence-Based Practice

Quality Improvement

Safety

Informatics

Buddy Review: _____   Faculty Review: _____

Grade Tracker

Related Exemplars

Related Concepts

Classroom Critical Thinking

Reading / Resources Critical Thinking

Priority Assessments

1
2
3

Priority Labs & Diagnostics

1
2
3

Priority Nursing Interventions

1
2
3

Priority Medications

1

2

3

Priority Potential & Actual Complications

1

2

3

Priority Collaborative Goals

1

2

3

NurseThink Quick

CARE ACCORDING TO THE NCLEX® TEST PLAN

Safe and Effective Care: Management of Care, Coordinated Care, Safety and Infection Control

Health Promotion and Maintenance

Psychosocial Integrity

Physiological Integrity: Basic Care and Comfort, Pharmacological and Parenteral Therapies, Reduction of Risk Potential, and Physiological Adaptation

CARE ACCORDING TO QUALITY AND SAFETY STANDARDS

Patient-Centered Care

Teamwork and Collaboration

Evidence-Based Practice

Quality Improvement

Safety

Informatics

Buddy Review: _____   Faculty Review: _____

Grade Tracker

Related Exemplars

Related Concepts

Classroom Critical Thinking

Reading / Resources Critical Thinking

Priority Assessments

1

2

3

Priority Labs & Diagnostics

1

2

3

Priority Nursing Interventions

1

2

3

Priority Medications

1

2

3

Priority Potential & Actual Complications

1

2

3

Priority Collaborative Goals

1

2

3

NurseThink Quick

CARE ACCORDING TO THE NCLEX® TEST PLAN

Safe and Effective Care: Management of Care, Coordinated Care, Safety and Infection Control

Health Promotion and Maintenance

Psychosocial Integrity

Physiological Integrity: Basic Care and Comfort, Pharmacological and Parenteral Therapies, Reduction of Risk Potential, and Physiological Adaptation

CARE ACCORDING TO QUALITY AND SAFETY STANDARDS

Patient-Centered Care

Teamwork and Collaboration

Evidence-Based Practice

Quality Improvement

Safety

Informatics

Buddy Review: _____   Faculty Review: _____

Grade Tracker

Related Exemplars

Related Concepts

Classroom Critical Thinking

Reading / Resources Critical Thinking

Priority Assessments

1
2
3

Priority Labs & Diagnostics

1
2
3

Priority Nursing Interventions

1
2
3

Priority Medications

1
2
3

**Priority Potential &
Actual Complications**

1
2
3

Priority Collaborative Goals

1
2
3

NurseThink Quick

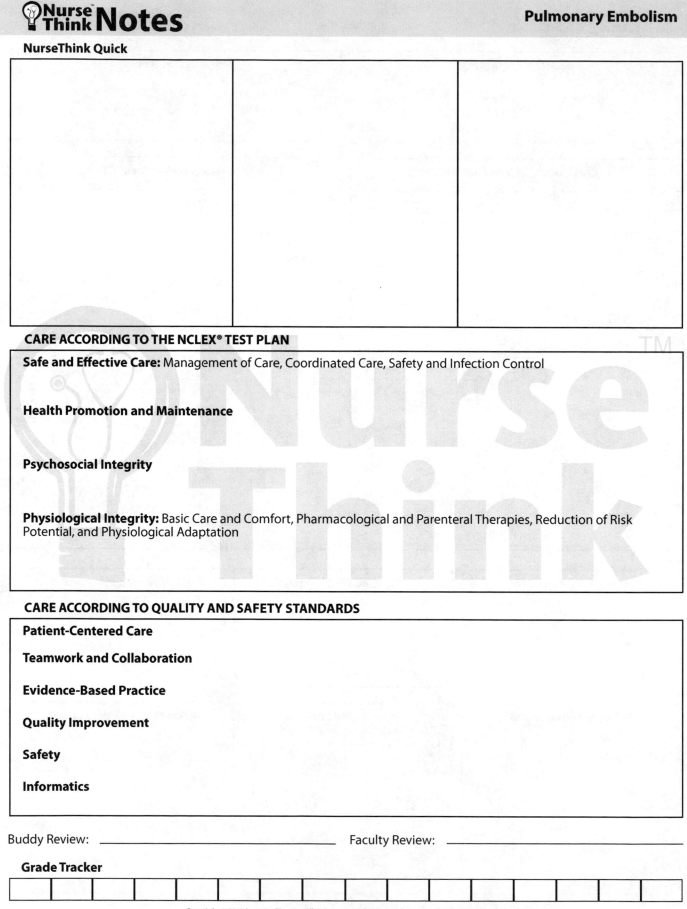

CARE ACCORDING TO THE NCLEX® TEST PLAN

Safe and Effective Care: Management of Care, Coordinated Care, Safety and Infection Control

Health Promotion and Maintenance

Psychosocial Integrity

Physiological Integrity: Basic Care and Comfort, Pharmacological and Parenteral Therapies, Reduction of Risk Potential, and Physiological Adaptation

CARE ACCORDING TO QUALITY AND SAFETY STANDARDS

Patient-Centered Care

Teamwork and Collaboration

Evidence-Based Practice

Quality Improvement

Safety

Informatics

Buddy Review: _____   Faculty Review: _____

Grade Tracker

Related Exemplars

Related Concepts

Classroom Critical Thinking

Reading / Resources Critical Thinking

Priority Assessments

1
2
3

Priority Labs & Diagnostics

1
2
3

Priority Nursing Interventions

1
2
3

Priority Medications

1
2
3

Priority Potential & Actual Complications

1
2
3

Priority Collaborative Goals

1
2
3

NurseThink Quick

CARE ACCORDING TO THE NCLEX® TEST PLAN

Safe and Effective Care: Management of Care, Coordinated Care, Safety and Infection Control

Health Promotion and Maintenance

Psychosocial Integrity

Physiological Integrity: Basic Care and Comfort, Pharmacological and Parenteral Therapies, Reduction of Risk Potential, and Physiological Adaptation

---

CARE ACCORDING TO QUALITY AND SAFETY STANDARDS

Patient-Centered Care

Teamwork and Collaboration

Evidence-Based Practice

Quality Improvement

Safety

Informatics

Buddy Review: _____   Faculty Review: _____

Grade Tracker

Related Exemplars

Related Concepts

Classroom Critical Thinking

Reading / Resources Critical Thinking

Priority Assessments

1
2
3

Priority Labs & Diagnostics

1
2
3

Priority Nursing Interventions

1
2
3

Priority Medications

1
2
3

Priority Potential & Actual Complications

1
2
3

Priority Collaborative Goals

1
2
3

NurseThink Quick

CARE ACCORDING TO THE NCLEX® TEST PLAN

Safe and Effective Care: Management of Care, Coordinated Care, Safety and Infection Control

Health Promotion and Maintenance

Psychosocial Integrity

Physiological Integrity: Basic Care and Comfort, Pharmacological and Parenteral Therapies, Reduction of Risk Potential, and Physiological Adaptation

CARE ACCORDING TO QUALITY AND SAFETY STANDARDS

Patient-Centered Care

Teamwork and Collaboration

Evidence-Based Practice

Quality Improvement

Safety

Informatics

Buddy Review: _____   Faculty Review: _____

Grade Tracker

 **Notes**

Related Exemplars	**Related Concepts**

Classroom Critical Thinking	**Reading / Resources Critical Thinking**

Priority Assessments

1

2

3

Priority Labs & Diagnostics

1

2

3

Priority Nursing Interventions

1

2

3

Priority Medications

1

2

3

Priority Potential & Actual Complications

1

2

3

Priority Collaborative Goals

1

2

3

NurseThink Quick

Cardiomyopathy: Categories
Hard
Hypertrophic
Arrhythmogenic right ventricular
Restrictive
Dilated

CARE ACCORDING TO THE NCLEX® TEST PLAN

Safe and Effective Care: Management of Care, Coordinated Care, Safety and Infection Control

Health Promotion and Maintenance

Psychosocial Integrity

Physiological Integrity: Basic Care and Comfort, Pharmacological and Parenteral Therapies, Reduction of Risk Potential, and Physiological Adaptation

CARE ACCORDING TO QUALITY AND SAFETY STANDARDS

Patient-Centered Care

Teamwork and Collaboration

Evidence-Based Practice

Quality Improvement

Safety

Informatics

Buddy Review: _____   Faculty Review: _____

Grade Tracker

 **Notes**

Heart Failure

Related Exemplars	Related Concepts

Classroom Critical Thinking	Reading / Resources Critical Thinking

Priority Assessments
1
2
3

Priority Labs & Diagnostics
1
2
3

Priority Nursing Interventions
1
2
3

Priority Medications
1
2
3

Priority Potential & Actual Complications
1
2
3

Priority Collaborative Goals
1
2
3

Copyright © 2017 by NurseTim, Inc. All rights reserved. No reproduction or distribution allowed.

NurseThink.com   Learn Right the First Time   65

NurseThink Quick

Digoxin Toxicity	Congestive Heart Failure: Treatment	CHF: Causes of Exacerbation
VANBAD	***Unload Fast***	***Failure***
Vomiting	**U**pright sitting	**F**orgot medication
Anorexia	**N**itroglycerine	**A**rrhythmia/Anemia
Nausea	**L**asix	**I**schemia/Infarction/Infection
Blurred vision	**O**xygen	**L**ifestyle: taken too much salt
Arrhythmias	**A**minophylline	**U**p regulation of cardiac output: pregnancy, hyperthyroidism
Diarrhea	**D**igoxin	**R**enal failure
	Fluids decrease	**E**mbolism: pulmonary
	Afterload decrease	
	Sodium decrease	
	Tests: digoxin Level, ABG, K+, BNP	

CARE ACCORDING TO THE NCLEX® TEST PLAN

Safe and Effective Care: Management of Care, Coordinated Care, Safety and Infection Control

Health Promotion and Maintenance

Psychosocial Integrity

Physiological Integrity: Basic Care and Comfort, Pharmacological and Parenteral Therapies, Reduction of Risk Potential, and Physiological Adaptation

CARE ACCORDING TO QUALITY AND SAFETY STANDARDS

Patient-Centered Care

Teamwork and Collaboration

Evidence-Based Practice

Quality Improvement

Safety

Informatics

Buddy Review: _____   Faculty Review: _____

Grade Tracker

Related Exemplars

Related Concepts

Classroom Critical Thinking

Reading / Resources Critical Thinking

Priority Assessments

1

2

3

Priority Labs & Diagnostics

1

2

3

Priority Nursing Interventions

1

2

3

Priority Medications

1

2

3

Priority Potential & Actual Complications

1

2

3

Priority Collaborative Goals

1

2

3

 **Notes**

NurseThink Quick

Hypertension Complications
4 C's
Coronary artery disease
Congestive heart failure
Chronic renal failure
Cardiovascular accident

Hypertension Treatment
ABCD
ACE inhibitors/AngII antagonists
Beta blockers
Calcium antagonists
Diuretics/Vasodilators

Hypertension Interventions
I-Tired
Intake and output
Transient ischemic attack (monitor)
Impaired perfusion monitoring
Respiration, pulse
Electrolytes
Daily weight

Hypertension: Secondary HTN Causes:
Chaps
Cushing's syndrome
Hyperaldosteronism
Aorta coarctation
Pheochromocytoma
Stenosis of renal arteries

CARE ACCORDING TO THE NCLEX® TEST PLAN

Safe and Effective Care: Management of Care, Coordinated Care, Safety and Infection Control

Health Promotion and Maintenance

Psychosocial Integrity

Physiological Integrity: Basic Care and Comfort, Pharmacological and Parenteral Therapies, Reduction of Risk Potential, and Physiological Adaptation

CARE ACCORDING TO QUALITY AND SAFETY STANDARDS

Patient-Centered Care

Teamwork and Collaboration

Evidence-Based Practice

Quality Improvement

Safety

Informatics

Buddy Review: _____ Faculty Review: _____

Grade Tracker

Related Exemplars	**Related Concepts**

Classroom Critical Thinking	**Reading / Resources Critical Thinking**

Priority Assessments	**Priority Labs & Diagnostics**	**Priority Nursing Interventions**
1	1	1
2	2	2
3	3	3

Priority Medications	**Priority Potential & Actual Complications**	**Priority Collaborative Goals**
1	1	1
2	2	2
3	3	3

NurseThink Quick

Myocardial Infarction: Signs and Symptoms

Pulse
Persistent chest pains
Upset stomach
Lightheadedness
Shortness of breath
Excessive sweating

Myocardial Infarction: Treatment

Monah
Morphine sulfate
Oxygen
Nitroglycerin
ASA
Heparin

MI: Complications

Leap on the Map
LVF
Embolism
Aneurysm
Progressive infarct
Myocardial rupture
Arrhythmias
Pericarditis

Myocardial Infarction: Management

Boomar
Bedrest
Oxygen
Opiate
Monitor
Anticoagulant
Reduce clot size

CARE ACCORDING TO THE NCLEX® TEST PLAN

Safe and Effective Care: Management of Care, Coordinated Care, Safety and Infection Control

Health Promotion and Maintenance

Psychosocial Integrity

Physiological Integrity: Basic Care and Comfort, Pharmacological and Parenteral Therapies, Reduction of Risk Potential, and Physiological Adaptation

CARE ACCORDING TO QUALITY AND SAFETY STANDARDS

Patient-Centered Care

Teamwork and Collaboration

Evidence-Based Practice

Quality Improvement

Safety

Informatics

Buddy Review: _____   Faculty Review: _____

Grade Tracker

Related Exemplars	**Related Concepts**

Classroom Critical Thinking	**Reading / Resources Critical Thinking**

Priority Assessments

1
2
3

Priority Labs & Diagnostics

1
2
3

Priority Nursing Interventions

1
2
3

Priority Medications

1

2

3

Priority Potential & Actual Complications

1

2

3

Priority Collaborative Goals

1

2

3

 **Notes**

NurseThink Quick

Aortic Stenosis Characteristics	**Mitral Stenosis (MS) vs. Regurgitation (MR)**	**Mitral Stenosis: Complications**
SAD	MS is a female predominant	**ABCED x 2**
Syncope	MR is male predominant	**A**rrhythmias/Aneurysm
Angina		**B**radycardia/Low BP
Dyspnea		**C**ardiac Failure/Cardiac tamponade
	Murmur Attributes	**D**resslers/Death
	IL PQRST	**E**mbolism
	Intensity	
	Location	
	Pitch	
	Quality	
	Radiation	
	Shape	
	Timing	

CARE ACCORDING TO THE NCLEX® TEST PLAN

Safe and Effective Care: Management of Care, Coordinated Care, Safety and Infection Control

Health Promotion and Maintenance

Psychosocial Integrity

Physiological Integrity: Basic Care and Comfort, Pharmacological and Parenteral Therapies, Reduction of Risk Potential, and Physiological Adaptation

CARE ACCORDING TO QUALITY AND SAFETY STANDARDS

Patient-Centered Care

Teamwork and Collaboration

Evidence-Based Practice

Quality Improvement

Safety

Informatics

Buddy Review: _____   Faculty Review: _____

Grade Tracker

Related Exemplars	Related Concepts

Classroom Critical Thinking	Reading / Resources Critical Thinking

Priority Assessments

1

2

3

Priority Labs & Diagnostics

1

2

3

Priority Nursing Interventions

1

2

3

Priority Medications

1

2

3

Priority Potential & Actual Complications

1

2

3

Priority Collaborative Goals

1

2

3

NurseThink Quick

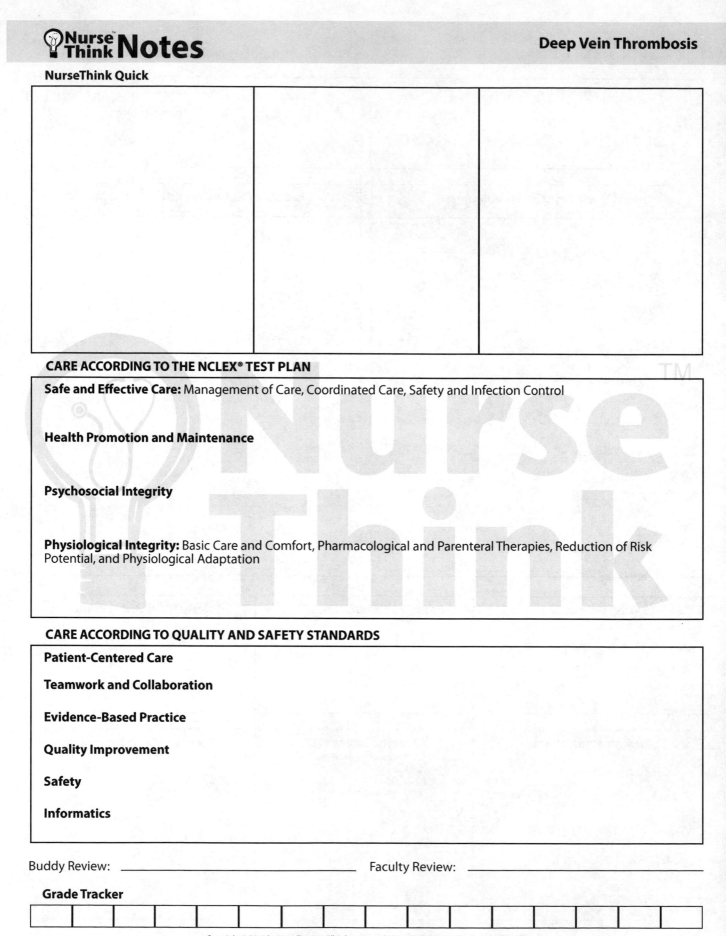

CARE ACCORDING TO THE NCLEX® TEST PLAN

Safe and Effective Care: Management of Care, Coordinated Care, Safety and Infection Control

Health Promotion and Maintenance

Psychosocial Integrity

Physiological Integrity: Basic Care and Comfort, Pharmacological and Parenteral Therapies, Reduction of Risk Potential, and Physiological Adaptation

CARE ACCORDING TO QUALITY AND SAFETY STANDARDS

Patient-Centered Care

Teamwork and Collaboration

Evidence-Based Practice

Quality Improvement

Safety

Informatics

Buddy Review: _____   Faculty Review: _____

Grade Tracker

Related Exemplars

Related Concepts

Classroom Critical Thinking

Reading / Resources Critical Thinking

Priority Assessments
1
2
3

Priority Labs & Diagnostics
1
2
3

Priority Nursing Interventions
1
2
3

Priority Medications
1
2
3

Priority Potential & Actual Complications
1
2
3

Priority Collaborative Goals
1
2
3

NurseThink Notes

NurseThink Quick

CARE ACCORDING TO THE NCLEX® TEST PLAN

Safe and Effective Care: Management of Care, Coordinated Care, Safety and Infection Control

Health Promotion and Maintenance

Psychosocial Integrity

Physiological Integrity: Basic Care and Comfort, Pharmacological and Parenteral Therapies, Reduction of Risk Potential, and Physiological Adaptation

CARE ACCORDING TO QUALITY AND SAFETY STANDARDS

Patient-Centered Care

Teamwork and Collaboration

Evidence-Based Practice

Quality Improvement

Safety

Informatics

Buddy Review: _____   Faculty Review: _____

Grade Tracker

Related Exemplars

Related Concepts

Classroom Critical Thinking

Reading / Resources Critical Thinking

Priority Assessments

1
2
3

Priority Labs & Diagnostics

1
2
3

Priority Nursing Interventions

1
2
3

Priority Medications

1
2
3

Priority Potential & Actual Complications

1
2
3

Priority Collaborative Goals

1
2
3

NurseThink Quick

CARE ACCORDING TO THE NCLEX® TEST PLAN

Safe and Effective Care: Management of Care, Coordinated Care, Safety and Infection Control

Health Promotion and Maintenance

Psychosocial Integrity

Physiological Integrity: Basic Care and Comfort, Pharmacological and Parenteral Therapies, Reduction of Risk Potential, and Physiological Adaptation

CARE ACCORDING TO QUALITY AND SAFETY STANDARDS

Patient-Centered Care

Teamwork and Collaboration

Evidence-Based Practice

Quality Improvement

Safety

Informatics

Buddy Review: _____   Faculty Review: _____

Grade Tracker

Related Exemplars

Related Concepts

Classroom Critical Thinking

Reading / Resources Critical Thinking

Priority Assessments

1
2
3

Priority Labs & Diagnostics

1
2
3

Priority Nursing Interventions

1
2
3

Priority Medications

1
2
3

Priority Potential & Actual Complications

1
2
3

Priority Collaborative Goals

1
2
3

NurseThink Quick

CARE ACCORDING TO THE NCLEX® TEST PLAN

Safe and Effective Care: Management of Care, Coordinated Care, Safety and Infection Control

Health Promotion and Maintenance

Psychosocial Integrity

Physiological Integrity: Basic Care and Comfort, Pharmacological and Parenteral Therapies, Reduction of Risk Potential, and Physiological Adaptation

CARE ACCORDING TO QUALITY AND SAFETY STANDARDS

Patient-Centered Care

Teamwork and Collaboration

Evidence-Based Practice

Quality Improvement

Safety

Informatics

Buddy Review: _____   Faculty Review: _____

Grade Tracker

Related Exemplars

Related Concepts

Classroom Critical Thinking

Reading / Resources Critical Thinking

Priority Assessments

1
2
3

Priority Labs & Diagnostics

1
2
3

Priority Nursing Interventions

1
2
3

Priority Medications

1
2
3

Priority Potential & Actual Complications

1
2
3

Priority Collaborative Goals

1
2
3

NurseThink Quick

CARE ACCORDING TO THE NCLEX® TEST PLAN

Safe and Effective Care: Management of Care, Coordinated Care, Safety and Infection Control

Health Promotion and Maintenance

Psychosocial Integrity

Physiological Integrity: Basic Care and Comfort, Pharmacological and Parenteral Therapies, Reduction of Risk Potential, and Physiological Adaptation

CARE ACCORDING TO QUALITY AND SAFETY STANDARDS

Patient-Centered Care

Teamwork and Collaboration

Evidence-Based Practice

Quality Improvement

Safety

Informatics

Buddy Review: _____   Faculty Review: _____

Grade Tracker

Related Exemplars	**Related Concepts**

Classroom Critical Thinking	**Reading / Resources Critical Thinking**

Priority Assessments

1

2

3

Priority Labs & Diagnostics

1

2

3

Priority Nursing Interventions

1

2

3

Priority Medications

1

2

3

Priority Potential & Actual Complications

1

2

3

Priority Collaborative Goals

1

2

3

NurseThink Notes

NurseThink Quick

CARE ACCORDING TO THE NCLEX® TEST PLAN

Safe and Effective Care: Management of Care, Coordinated Care, Safety and Infection Control

Health Promotion and Maintenance

Psychosocial Integrity

Physiological Integrity: Basic Care and Comfort, Pharmacological and Parenteral Therapies, Reduction of Risk Potential, and Physiological Adaptation

CARE ACCORDING TO QUALITY AND SAFETY STANDARDS

Patient-Centered Care

Teamwork and Collaboration

Evidence-Based Practice

Quality Improvement

Safety

Informatics

Buddy Review: _____   Faculty Review: _____

Grade Tracker

Related Exemplars	**Related Concepts**

Classroom Critical Thinking	**Reading / Resources Critical Thinking**

Priority Assessments

1
2
3

Priority Labs & Diagnostics

1
2
3

Priority Nursing Interventions

1
2
3

Priority Medications

1
2
3

Priority Potential & Actual Complications

1
2
3

Priority Collaborative Goals

1
2
3

NurseThink Quick

CARE ACCORDING TO THE NCLEX® TEST PLAN

Safe and Effective Care: Management of Care, Coordinated Care, Safety and Infection Control

Health Promotion and Maintenance

Psychosocial Integrity

Physiological Integrity: Basic Care and Comfort, Pharmacological and Parenteral Therapies, Reduction of Risk Potential, and Physiological Adaptation

CARE ACCORDING TO QUALITY AND SAFETY STANDARDS

Patient-Centered Care

Teamwork and Collaboration

Evidence-Based Practice

Quality Improvement

Safety

Informatics

Buddy Review: _____   Faculty Review: _____

Grade Tracker

Related Exemplars	Related Concepts

Classroom Critical Thinking	Reading / Resources Critical Thinking

Priority Assessments	Priority Labs & Diagnostics	Priority Nursing Interventions
1	1	1
2	2	2
3	3	3

Priority Medications	Priority Potential & Actual Complications	Priority Collaborative Goals
1	1	1
2	2	2
3	3	3

NurseThink Notes

NurseThink Quick

CARE ACCORDING TO THE NCLEX® TEST PLAN

Safe and Effective Care: Management of Care, Coordinated Care, Safety and Infection Control

Health Promotion and Maintenance

Psychosocial Integrity

Physiological Integrity: Basic Care and Comfort, Pharmacological and Parenteral Therapies, Reduction of Risk Potential, and Physiological Adaptation

CARE ACCORDING TO QUALITY AND SAFETY STANDARDS

Patient-Centered Care

Teamwork and Collaboration

Evidence-Based Practice

Quality Improvement

Safety

Informatics

Buddy Review: _____   Faculty Review: _____

Grade Tracker

Related Exemplars

Related Concepts

Classroom Critical Thinking

Reading / Resources Critical Thinking

Priority Assessments

1

2

3

Priority Labs & Diagnostics

1

2

3

Priority Nursing Interventions

1

2

3

Priority Medications

1

2

3

Priority Potential & Actual Complications

1

2

3

Priority Collaborative Goals

1

2

3

NurseThink Quick

CARE ACCORDING TO THE NCLEX® TEST PLAN

Safe and Effective Care: Management of Care, Coordinated Care, Safety and Infection Control

Health Promotion and Maintenance

Psychosocial Integrity

Physiological Integrity: Basic Care and Comfort, Pharmacological and Parenteral Therapies, Reduction of Risk Potential, and Physiological Adaptation

CARE ACCORDING TO QUALITY AND SAFETY STANDARDS

Patient-Centered Care

Teamwork and Collaboration

Evidence-Based Practice

Quality Improvement

Safety

Informatics

Buddy Review: _____   Faculty Review: _____

Grade Tracker

Related Exemplars	**Related Concepts**

Classroom Critical Thinking	**Reading / Resources Critical Thinking**

Priority Assessments

1
2
3

Priority Labs & Diagnostics

1
2
3

Priority Nursing Interventions

1
2
3

Priority Medications

1

2

3

Priority Potential & Actual Complications

1

2

3

Priority Collaborative Goals

1

2

3

NurseThink Quick

CARE ACCORDING TO THE NCLEX® TEST PLAN

Safe and Effective Care: Management of Care, Coordinated Care, Safety and Infection Control

Health Promotion and Maintenance

Psychosocial Integrity

Physiological Integrity: Basic Care and Comfort, Pharmacological and Parenteral Therapies, Reduction of Risk Potential, and Physiological Adaptation

CARE ACCORDING TO QUALITY AND SAFETY STANDARDS

Patient-Centered Care

Teamwork and Collaboration

Evidence-Based Practice

Quality Improvement

Safety

Informatics

Buddy Review: _____   Faculty Review: _____

Grade Tracker

Related Exemplars	Related Concepts

Classroom Critical Thinking	Reading / Resources Critical Thinking

Priority Assessments

1
2
3

Priority Labs & Diagnostics

1
2
3

Priority Nursing Interventions

1
2
3

Priority Medications

1
2
3

Priority Potential & Actual Complications

1
2
3

Priority Collaborative Goals

1
2
3

NurseThink Quick

CARE ACCORDING TO THE NCLEX® TEST PLAN

Safe and Effective Care: Management of Care, Coordinated Care, Safety and Infection Control

Health Promotion and Maintenance

Psychosocial Integrity

Physiological Integrity: Basic Care and Comfort, Pharmacological and Parenteral Therapies, Reduction of Risk Potential, and Physiological Adaptation

CARE ACCORDING TO QUALITY AND SAFETY STANDARDS

Patient-Centered Care

Teamwork and Collaboration

Evidence-Based Practice

Quality Improvement

Safety

Informatics

Buddy Review: _____   Faculty Review: _____

Grade Tracker

Related Exemplars	**Related Concepts**

Classroom Critical Thinking	**Reading / Resources Critical Thinking**

Priority Assessments

1
2
3

Priority Labs & Diagnostics

1
2
3

Priority Nursing Interventions

1
2
3

Priority Medications

1

2

3

Priority Potential & Actual Complications

1

2

3

Priority Collaborative Goals

1

2

3

NurseThink Quick

CARE ACCORDING TO THE NCLEX® TEST PLAN

Safe and Effective Care: Management of Care, Coordinated Care, Safety and Infection Control

Health Promotion and Maintenance

Psychosocial Integrity

Physiological Integrity: Basic Care and Comfort, Pharmacological and Parenteral Therapies, Reduction of Risk Potential, and Physiological Adaptation

CARE ACCORDING TO QUALITY AND SAFETY STANDARDS

Patient-Centered Care

Teamwork and Collaboration

Evidence-Based Practice

Quality Improvement

Safety

Informatics

Buddy Review: _____   Faculty Review: _____

Grade Tracker

Related Exemplars

Related Concepts

Classroom Critical Thinking

Reading / Resources Critical Thinking

Priority Assessments

1

2

3

Priority Labs & Diagnostics

1

2

3

Priority Nursing Interventions

1

2

3

Priority Medications

1

2

3

Priority Potential & Actual Complications

1

2

3

Priority Collaborative Goals

1

2

3

NurseThink Quick

CARE ACCORDING TO THE NCLEX® TEST PLAN

Safe and Effective Care: Management of Care, Coordinated Care, Safety and Infection Control

Health Promotion and Maintenance

Psychosocial Integrity

Physiological Integrity: Basic Care and Comfort, Pharmacological and Parenteral Therapies, Reduction of Risk Potential, and Physiological Adaptation

CARE ACCORDING TO QUALITY AND SAFETY STANDARDS

Patient-Centered Care

Teamwork and Collaboration

Evidence-Based Practice

Quality Improvement

Safety

Informatics

Buddy Review: _____   Faculty Review: _____

Grade Tracker

Related Exemplars

Related Concepts

Classroom Critical Thinking

Reading / Resources Critical Thinking

Priority Assessments

1
2
3

Priority Labs & Diagnostics

1
2
3

Priority Nursing Interventions

1
2
3

Priority Medications

1
2
3

Priority Potential & Actual Complications

1
2
3

Priority Collaborative Goals

1
2
3

NurseThink Quick

<table>
<tr><td></td><td></td><td></td></tr>
</table>

CARE ACCORDING TO THE NCLEX® TEST PLAN

Safe and Effective Care: Management of Care, Coordinated Care, Safety and Infection Control

Health Promotion and Maintenance

Psychosocial Integrity

Physiological Integrity: Basic Care and Comfort, Pharmacological and Parenteral Therapies, Reduction of Risk Potential, and Physiological Adaptation

CARE ACCORDING TO QUALITY AND SAFETY STANDARDS

Patient-Centered Care

Teamwork and Collaboration

Evidence-Based Practice

Quality Improvement

Safety

Informatics

Buddy Review: _____   Faculty Review: _____

Grade Tracker

<table>
<tr><td></td><td></td><td></td><td></td><td></td><td></td><td></td><td></td><td></td><td></td><td></td><td></td><td></td><td></td><td></td><td></td></tr>
</table>

Related Exemplars

Related Concepts

Classroom Critical Thinking

Reading / Resources Critical Thinking

Priority Assessments

1
2
3

Priority Labs & Diagnostics

1
2
3

Priority Nursing Interventions

1
2
3

Priority Medications

1
2
3

Priority Potential & Actual Complications

1
2
3

Priority Collaborative Goals

1
2
3

NurseThink Quick

CARE ACCORDING TO THE NCLEX® TEST PLAN

Safe and Effective Care: Management of Care, Coordinated Care, Safety and Infection Control

Health Promotion and Maintenance

Psychosocial Integrity

Physiological Integrity: Basic Care and Comfort, Pharmacological and Parenteral Therapies, Reduction of Risk Potential, and Physiological Adaptation

CARE ACCORDING TO QUALITY AND SAFETY STANDARDS

Patient-Centered Care

Teamwork and Collaboration

Evidence-Based Practice

Quality Improvement

Safety

Informatics

Buddy Review: _____   Faculty Review: _____

Grade Tracker

Related Exemplars

Related Concepts

Classroom Critical Thinking

Reading / Resources Critical Thinking

Priority Assessments

1
2
3

Priority Labs & Diagnostics

1
2
3

Priority Nursing Interventions

1
2
3

Priority Medications

1
2
3

Priority Potential & Actual Complications

1
2
3

Priority Collaborative Goals

1
2
3

NurseThink Quick

CARE ACCORDING TO THE NCLEX® TEST PLAN

Safe and Effective Care: Management of Care, Coordinated Care, Safety and Infection Control

Health Promotion and Maintenance

Psychosocial Integrity

Physiological Integrity: Basic Care and Comfort, Pharmacological and Parenteral Therapies, Reduction of Risk Potential, and Physiological Adaptation

CARE ACCORDING TO QUALITY AND SAFETY STANDARDS

Patient-Centered Care

Teamwork and Collaboration

Evidence-Based Practice

Quality Improvement

Safety

Informatics

Buddy Review: _____   Faculty Review: _____

Grade Tracker

Related Exemplars	Related Concepts

Classroom Critical Thinking	Reading / Resources Critical Thinking

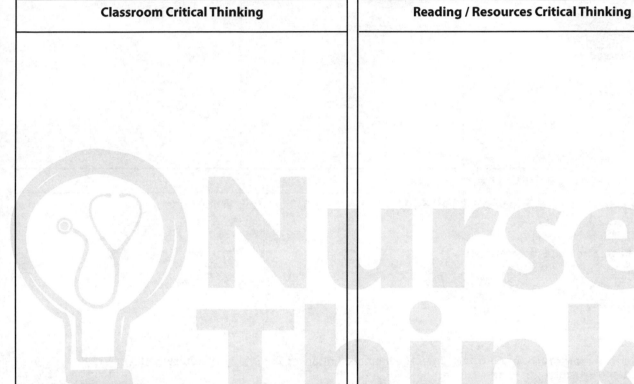

Priority Assessments

1

2

3

Priority Labs & Diagnostics

1

2

3

Priority Nursing Interventions

1

2

3

Priority Medications

1

2

3

Priority Potential & Actual Complications

1

2

3

Priority Collaborative Goals

1

2

3

NurseThink Notes

NurseThink Quick

Altered Mental State: Causes	Confusion: Causes	
AEIOU Tips **A**lcohol/Drugs **E**ndocrine **I**nsulin **U**remia **O**verdose **T**oxins/Trauma/Tumor **I**nfections **P**sychosis/Porphyria **S**troke/Seizure/Shock	**Dim Face** **D**rugs Dehydration **I**nfection **M**etabolic/MI **F**racture/Failure **A**lcohol/Anemia **C**VA **E**lectrolyte disturbances	

CARE ACCORDING TO THE NCLEX® TEST PLAN

Safe and Effective Care: Management of Care, Coordinated Care, Safety and Infection Control

Health Promotion and Maintenance

Psychosocial Integrity

Physiological Integrity: Basic Care and Comfort, Pharmacological and Parenteral Therapies, Reduction of Risk Potential, and Physiological Adaptation

CARE ACCORDING TO QUALITY AND SAFETY STANDARDS

Patient-Centered Care

Teamwork and Collaboration

Evidence-Based Practice

Quality Improvement

Safety

Informatics

Buddy Review: _____   Faculty Review: _____

Grade Tracker

Related Exemplars

Related Concepts

Classroom Critical Thinking

Reading / Resources Critical Thinking

Priority Assessments

1

2

3

Priority Labs & Diagnostics

1

2

3

Priority Nursing Interventions

1

2

3

Priority Medications

1

2

3

Priority Potential & Actual Complications

1

2

3

Priority Collaborative Goals

1

2

3

NurseThink Quick

Dementia: Causes	**Alzheimer's Disease: Progressive Phases**	
Dementia		
Drugs and alcohol (including over-the-counter drugs)	***ABCD***	
Eyes and ears (disorientation due to visual/auditory distortion)	**A**mnesic phase (forgetting)	
Medical disorders (diabetes, hypothyroidism)	**B**ehavioral problems (antisocial, wandering)	
Emotional and psychological disturbances (mood or paranoid disorders)	**C**ortical phase (incontinence, falls)	
Neurological disorders (multiinfarct dementia)	**D**ecerebrate phase (return to primitive reflexes)	
Tumors and trauma		
Infections (urinary tract or upper respiratory tract)		
Arteriosclerosis (leading to heart failure, insufficient blood supply to heart and brain, and confusion)		

CARE ACCORDING TO THE NCLEX® TEST PLAN

Safe and Effective Care: Management of Care, Coordinated Care, Safety and Infection Control

Health Promotion and Maintenance

Psychosocial Integrity

Physiological Integrity: Basic Care and Comfort, Pharmacological and Parenteral Therapies, Reduction of Risk Potential, and Physiological Adaptation

CARE ACCORDING TO QUALITY AND SAFETY STANDARDS

Patient-Centered Care

Teamwork and Collaboration

Evidence-Based Practice

Quality Improvement

Safety

Informatics

Buddy Review: _____   Faculty Review: _____

Grade Tracker

Related Exemplars	**Related Concepts**

Classroom Critical Thinking	**Reading / Resources Critical Thinking**

Priority Assessments	**Priority Labs & Diagnostics**	**Priority Nursing Interventions**
1	1	1
2	2	2
3	3	3

Priority Medications	**Priority Potential & Actual Complications**	**Priority Collaborative Goals**
1	1	1
2	2	2
3	3	3

NurseThink Quick

CARE ACCORDING TO THE NCLEX® TEST PLAN

Safe and Effective Care: Management of Care, Coordinated Care, Safety and Infection Control

Health Promotion and Maintenance

Psychosocial Integrity

Physiological Integrity: Basic Care and Comfort, Pharmacological and Parenteral Therapies, Reduction of Risk Potential, and Physiological Adaptation

CARE ACCORDING TO QUALITY AND SAFETY STANDARDS

Patient-Centered Care

Teamwork and Collaboration

Evidence-Based Practice

Quality Improvement

Safety

Informatics

Buddy Review: _____   Faculty Review: _____

Grade Tracker

Related Exemplars

Related Concepts

Classroom Critical Thinking

Reading / Resources Critical Thinking

Priority Assessments

1
2
3

Priority Labs & Diagnostics

1
2
3

Priority Nursing Interventions

1
2
3

Priority Medications

1
2
3

Priority Potential & Actual Complications

1
2
3

Priority Collaborative Goals

1
2
3

NurseThink Quick

CARE ACCORDING TO THE NCLEX® TEST PLAN

Safe and Effective Care: Management of Care, Coordinated Care, Safety and Infection Control

Health Promotion and Maintenance

Psychosocial Integrity

Physiological Integrity: Basic Care and Comfort, Pharmacological and Parenteral Therapies, Reduction of Risk Potential, and Physiological Adaptation

CARE ACCORDING TO QUALITY AND SAFETY STANDARDS

Patient-Centered Care

Teamwork and Collaboration

Evidence-Based Practice

Quality Improvement

Safety

Informatics

Buddy Review: _____   Faculty Review: _____

Grade Tracker

Related Exemplars	Related Concepts

Classroom Critical Thinking	Reading / Resources Critical Thinking

Priority Assessments

1

2

3

Priority Labs & Diagnostics

1

2

3

Priority Nursing Interventions

1

2

3

Priority Medications

1

2

3

Priority Potential & Actual Complications

1

2

3

Priority Collaborative Goals

1

2

3

NurseThink Quick

CARE ACCORDING TO THE NCLEX® TEST PLAN

Safe and Effective Care: Management of Care, Coordinated Care, Safety and Infection Control

Health Promotion and Maintenance

Psychosocial Integrity

Physiological Integrity: Basic Care and Comfort, Pharmacological and Parenteral Therapies, Reduction of Risk Potential, and Physiological Adaptation

CARE ACCORDING TO QUALITY AND SAFETY STANDARDS

Patient-Centered Care

Teamwork and Collaboration

Evidence-Based Practice

Quality Improvement

Safety

Informatics

Buddy Review: _____   Faculty Review: _____

Grade Tracker

Related Exemplars	**Related Concepts**

Classroom Critical Thinking	**Reading / Resources Critical Thinking**

Priority Assessments

1
2
3

Priority Labs & Diagnostics

1
2
3

Priority Nursing Interventions

1
2
3

Priority Medications

1

2

3

Priority Potential & Actual Complications

1

2

3

Priority Collaborative Goals

1

2

3

NurseThink Quick

CARE ACCORDING TO THE NCLEX® TEST PLAN

Safe and Effective Care: Management of Care, Coordinated Care, Safety and Infection Control

Health Promotion and Maintenance

Psychosocial Integrity

Physiological Integrity: Basic Care and Comfort, Pharmacological and Parenteral Therapies, Reduction of Risk Potential, and Physiological Adaptation

CARE ACCORDING TO QUALITY AND SAFETY STANDARDS

Patient-Centered Care

Teamwork and Collaboration

Evidence-Based Practice

Quality Improvement

Safety

Informatics

Buddy Review: _____   Faculty Review: _____

Grade Tracker

Related Exemplars	Related Concepts

Classroom Critical Thinking	Reading / Resources Critical Thinking

Priority Assessments

1
2
3

Priority Labs & Diagnostics

1
2
3

Priority Nursing Interventions

1
2
3

Priority Medications

1

2

3

Priority Potential & Actual Complications

1

2

3

Priority Collaborative Goals

1

2

3

NurseThink Quick

CARE ACCORDING TO THE NCLEX® TEST PLAN

Safe and Effective Care: Management of Care, Coordinated Care, Safety and Infection Control

Health Promotion and Maintenance

Psychosocial Integrity

Physiological Integrity: Basic Care and Comfort, Pharmacological and Parenteral Therapies, Reduction of Risk Potential, and Physiological Adaptation

CARE ACCORDING TO QUALITY AND SAFETY STANDARDS

Patient-Centered Care

Teamwork and Collaboration

Evidence-Based Practice

Quality Improvement

Safety

Informatics

Buddy Review: _____   Faculty Review: _____

Grade Tracker

Related Exemplars	**Related Concepts**

Classroom Critical Thinking	**Reading / Resources Critical Thinking**

Priority Assessments

1
2
3

Priority Labs & Diagnostics

1
2
3

Priority Nursing Interventions

1
2
3

Priority Medications

1

2

3

Priority Potential & Actual Complications

1

2

3

Priority Collaborative Goals

1

2

3

NurseThink Quick

CARE ACCORDING TO THE NCLEX® TEST PLAN

Safe and Effective Care: Management of Care, Coordinated Care, Safety and Infection Control

Health Promotion and Maintenance

Psychosocial Integrity

Physiological Integrity: Basic Care and Comfort, Pharmacological and Parenteral Therapies, Reduction of Risk Potential, and Physiological Adaptation

CARE ACCORDING TO QUALITY AND SAFETY STANDARDS

Patient-Centered Care

Teamwork and Collaboration

Evidence-Based Practice

Quality Improvement

Safety

Informatics

Buddy Review: _____   Faculty Review: _____

Grade Tracker

Related Exemplars	Related Concepts

Classroom Critical Thinking	Reading / Resources Critical Thinking

Priority Assessments	Priority Labs & Diagnostics	Priority Nursing Interventions
1	1	1
2	2	2
3	3	3

Priority Medications	Priority Potential & Actual Complications	Priority Collaborative Goals
1	1	1
2	2	2
3	3	3

NurseThink Quick

Pruritus: Systemic Causes		
Itch **I**ron deficiency anemia/Internal malignancy **T**hyroid disease/Type I DM **C**hronic renal failure/Chronic liver disease **H**IV infection/Hereditary hemochromatosis		

CARE ACCORDING TO THE NCLEX® TEST PLAN

Safe and Effective Care: Management of Care, Coordinated Care, Safety and Infection Control

Health Promotion and Maintenance

Psychosocial Integrity

Physiological Integrity: Basic Care and Comfort, Pharmacological and Parenteral Therapies, Reduction of Risk Potential, and Physiological Adaptation

CARE ACCORDING TO QUALITY AND SAFETY STANDARDS

Patient-Centered Care

Teamwork and Collaboration

Evidence-Based Practice

Quality Improvement

Safety

Informatics

Buddy Review: _____   Faculty Review: _____

Grade Tracker

Related Exemplars

Related Concepts

Classroom Critical Thinking

Reading / Resources Critical Thinking

Priority Assessments

1
2
3

Priority Labs & Diagnostics

1
2
3

Priority Nursing Interventions

1
2
3

Priority Medications

1
2
3

Priority Potential & Actual Complications

1
2
3

Priority Collaborative Goals

1
2
3

NurseThink Quick

CARE ACCORDING TO THE NCLEX® TEST PLAN

Safe and Effective Care: Management of Care, Coordinated Care, Safety and Infection Control

Health Promotion and Maintenance

Psychosocial Integrity

Physiological Integrity: Basic Care and Comfort, Pharmacological and Parenteral Therapies, Reduction of Risk Potential, and Physiological Adaptation

CARE ACCORDING TO QUALITY AND SAFETY STANDARDS

Patient-Centered Care

Teamwork and Collaboration

Evidence-Based Practice

Quality Improvement

Safety

Informatics

Buddy Review: _____   Faculty Review: _____

Grade Tracker

Related Exemplars	Related Concepts

Classroom Critical Thinking	Reading / Resources Critical Thinking

Priority Assessments	Priority Labs & Diagnostics	Priority Nursing Interventions
1	1	1
2	2	2
3	3	3

Priority Medications	Priority Potential & Actual Complications	Priority Collaborative Goals
1	1	1
2	2	2
3	3	3

NurseThink Quick

Pressure Sore: Norton Score		
Magic **M**obility **A**DL **G**eneral condition **I**ncontinence **C**onscious level		

CARE ACCORDING TO THE NCLEX® TEST PLAN

Safe and Effective Care: Management of Care, Coordinated Care, Safety and Infection Control

Health Promotion and Maintenance

Psychosocial Integrity

Physiological Integrity: Basic Care and Comfort, Pharmacological and Parenteral Therapies, Reduction of Risk Potential, and Physiological Adaptation

CARE ACCORDING TO QUALITY AND SAFETY STANDARDS

Patient-Centered Care

Teamwork and Collaboration

Evidence-Based Practice

Quality Improvement

Safety

Informatics

Buddy Review: _____   Faculty Review: _____

Grade Tracker

Related Exemplars

Related Concepts

Classroom Critical Thinking

Reading / Resources Critical Thinking

Priority Assessments

1

2

3

Priority Labs & Diagnostics

1

2

3

Priority Nursing Interventions

1

2

3

Priority Medications

1

2

3

Priority Potential & Actual Complications

1

2

3

Priority Collaborative Goals

1

2

3

NurseThink Quick

CARE ACCORDING TO THE NCLEX® TEST PLAN

Safe and Effective Care: Management of Care, Coordinated Care, Safety and Infection Control

Health Promotion and Maintenance

Psychosocial Integrity

Physiological Integrity: Basic Care and Comfort, Pharmacological and Parenteral Therapies, Reduction of Risk Potential, and Physiological Adaptation

CARE ACCORDING TO QUALITY AND SAFETY STANDARDS

Patient-Centered Care

Teamwork and Collaboration

Evidence-Based Practice

Quality Improvement

Safety

Informatics

Buddy Review: _____   Faculty Review: _____

Grade Tracker

 **Notes**

Bereavement

Related Exemplars

Related Concepts

Classroom Critical Thinking

Reading / Resources Critical Thinking

Priority Assessments

1

2

3

Priority Labs & Diagnostics

1

2

3

Priority Nursing Interventions

1

2

3

Priority Medications

1

2

3

Priority Potential & Actual Complications

1

2

3

Priority Collaborative Goals

1

2

3

NurseThink Quick

CARE ACCORDING TO THE NCLEX® TEST PLAN

Safe and Effective Care: Management of Care, Coordinated Care, Safety and Infection Control

Health Promotion and Maintenance

Psychosocial Integrity

Physiological Integrity: Basic Care and Comfort, Pharmacological and Parenteral Therapies, Reduction of Risk Potential, and Physiological Adaptation

CARE ACCORDING TO QUALITY AND SAFETY STANDARDS

Patient-Centered Care

Teamwork and Collaboration

Evidence-Based Practice

Quality Improvement

Safety

Informatics

Buddy Review: _____   Faculty Review: _____

Grade Tracker

Related Exemplars

Related Concepts

Classroom Critical Thinking

Reading / Resources Critical Thinking

Priority Assessments

1
2
3

Priority Labs & Diagnostics

1
2
3

Priority Nursing Interventions

1
2
3

Priority Medications

1
2
3

Priority Potential & Actual Complications

1
2
3

Priority Collaborative Goals

1
2
3

NurseThink Notes

NurseThink Quick

CARE ACCORDING TO THE NCLEX® TEST PLAN

Safe and Effective Care: Management of Care, Coordinated Care, Safety and Infection Control

Health Promotion and Maintenance

Psychosocial Integrity

Physiological Integrity: Basic Care and Comfort, Pharmacological and Parenteral Therapies, Reduction of Risk Potential, and Physiological Adaptation

CARE ACCORDING TO QUALITY AND SAFETY STANDARDS

Patient-Centered Care

Teamwork and Collaboration

Evidence-Based Practice

Quality Improvement

Safety

Informatics

Buddy Review: _____   Faculty Review: _____

Grade Tracker

Related Exemplars	Related Concepts

Classroom Critical Thinking	Reading / Resources Critical Thinking

Priority Assessments

1
2
3

Priority Labs & Diagnostics

1
2
3

Priority Nursing Interventions

1
2
3

Priority Medications

1

2

3

Priority Potential & Actual Complications

1

2

3

Priority Collaborative Goals

1

2

3

NurseThink Quick

CARE ACCORDING TO THE NCLEX® TEST PLAN

Safe and Effective Care: Management of Care, Coordinated Care, Safety and Infection Control

Health Promotion and Maintenance

Psychosocial Integrity

Physiological Integrity: Basic Care and Comfort, Pharmacological and Parenteral Therapies, Reduction of Risk Potential, and Physiological Adaptation

CARE ACCORDING TO QUALITY AND SAFETY STANDARDS

Patient-Centered Care

Teamwork and Collaboration

Evidence-Based Practice

Quality Improvement

Safety

Informatics

Buddy Review: _____   Faculty Review: _____

Grade Tracker

Related Exemplars	**Related Concepts**

Classroom Critical Thinking	**Reading / Resources Critical Thinking**

Priority Assessments	**Priority Labs & Diagnostics**	**Priority Nursing Interventions**
1	1	1
2	2	2
3	3	3

Priority Medications	**Priority Potential & Actual Complications**	**Priority Collaborative Goals**
1	1	1
2	2	2
3	3	3

NurseThink Quick

CARE ACCORDING TO THE NCLEX® TEST PLAN

Safe and Effective Care: Management of Care, Coordinated Care, Safety and Infection Control

Health Promotion and Maintenance

Psychosocial Integrity

Physiological Integrity: Basic Care and Comfort, Pharmacological and Parenteral Therapies, Reduction of Risk Potential, and Physiological Adaptation

CARE ACCORDING TO QUALITY AND SAFETY STANDARDS

Patient-Centered Care

Teamwork and Collaboration

Evidence-Based Practice

Quality Improvement

Safety

Informatics

Buddy Review: _____   Faculty Review: _____

Grade Tracker

Related Exemplars	Related Concepts

Classroom Critical Thinking	Reading / Resources Critical Thinking

Priority Assessments

1
2
3

Priority Labs & Diagnostics

1
2
3

Priority Nursing Interventions

1
2
3

Priority Medications

1

2

3

Priority Potential & Actual Complications

1

2

3

Priority Collaborative Goals

1

2

3

NurseThink Quick

CARE ACCORDING TO THE NCLEX® TEST PLAN

Safe and Effective Care: Management of Care, Coordinated Care, Safety and Infection Control

Health Promotion and Maintenance

Psychosocial Integrity

Physiological Integrity: Basic Care and Comfort, Pharmacological and Parenteral Therapies, Reduction of Risk Potential, and Physiological Adaptation

CARE ACCORDING TO QUALITY AND SAFETY STANDARDS

Patient-Centered Care

Teamwork and Collaboration

Evidence-Based Practice

Quality Improvement

Safety

Informatics

Buddy Review: _____   Faculty Review: _____

Grade Tracker

Related Exemplars	Related Concepts

Classroom Critical Thinking	Reading / Resources Critical Thinking

Priority Assessments

1
2
3

Priority Labs & Diagnostics

1
2
3

Priority Nursing Interventions

1
2
3

Priority Medications

1

2

3

Priority Potential & Actual Complications

1

2

3

Priority Collaborative Goals

1

2

3

NurseThink Quick

CARE ACCORDING TO THE NCLEX® TEST PLAN

Safe and Effective Care: Management of Care, Coordinated Care, Safety and Infection Control

Health Promotion and Maintenance

Psychosocial Integrity

Physiological Integrity: Basic Care and Comfort, Pharmacological and Parenteral Therapies, Reduction of Risk Potential, and Physiological Adaptation

CARE ACCORDING TO QUALITY AND SAFETY STANDARDS

Patient-Centered Care

Teamwork and Collaboration

Evidence-Based Practice

Quality Improvement

Safety

Informatics

Buddy Review: _____   Faculty Review: _____

Grade Tracker

Related Exemplars	Related Concepts

Classroom Critical Thinking	Reading / Resources Critical Thinking

Priority Assessments

1
2
3

Priority Labs & Diagnostics

1
2
3

Priority Nursing Interventions

1
2
3

Priority Medications

1
2
3

Priority Potential & Actual Complications

1
2
3

Priority Collaborative Goals

1
2
3

NurseThink Notes

Concept: Homeostasis - Acid-Base, Fluid, Electrolytes

NurseThink Quick

Alkalosis and Acidosis
Alkalosis - has a "k" - kicking the pH up
Acidosis - has a "d" - dropping the pH down

ABG Analysis
Rome
Respiratory
Opposite
Metabolic
Equal

Solutions: Isotonic, Hypotonic, Hypertonic
Isotonic - "same as I" - the solution used will be the same as normal body fluid composition. Fluids remain inside intravascular space.
Hypotonic - "hypo, hippo" - the solution pulls fluid from the intravascular space into the ICF - the cell "swells like a hippo."

Acid-Base Balance
Respiratory: Opposite
ph>7.45 & pco2<35 = respiratory alkalosis
ph<7.35 & pco2>45 = respiratory acidosis
Metabolic: Equal
ph>7.45 & hco3>26 = metabolic alkalosis
ph<7.35 & hco3<22 = metabolic acidosis

CARE ACCORDING TO THE NCLEX® TEST PLAN

Safe and Effective Care: Management of Care, Coordinated Care, Safety and Infection Control

Health Promotion and Maintenance

Psychosocial Integrity

Physiological Integrity: Basic Care and Comfort, Pharmacological and Parenteral Therapies, Reduction of Risk Potential, and Physiological Adaptation

CARE ACCORDING TO QUALITY AND SAFETY STANDARDS

Patient-Centered Care

Teamwork and Collaboration

Evidence-Based Practice

Quality Improvement

Safety

Informatics

Buddy Review: _____   Faculty Review: _____

Grade Tracker

NurseThink Notes

Related Exemplars	**Related Concepts**

Classroom Critical Thinking	**Reading / Resources Critical Thinking**

Priority Assessments

1

2

3

Priority Labs & Diagnostics

1

2

3

Priority Nursing Interventions

1

2

3

Priority Medications

1

2

3

Priority Potential & Actual Complications

1

2

3

Priority Collaborative Goals

1

2

3

NurseThink Notes

NurseThink Quick

CARE ACCORDING TO THE NCLEX® TEST PLAN

Safe and Effective Care: Management of Care, Coordinated Care, Safety and Infection Control

Health Promotion and Maintenance

Psychosocial Integrity

Physiological Integrity: Basic Care and Comfort, Pharmacological and Parenteral Therapies, Reduction of Risk Potential, and Physiological Adaptation

CARE ACCORDING TO QUALITY AND SAFETY STANDARDS

Patient-Centered Care

Teamwork and Collaboration

Evidence-Based Practice

Quality Improvement

Safety

Informatics

Buddy Review: _____   Faculty Review: _____

Grade Tracker

Related Exemplars	Related Concepts

Classroom Critical Thinking	Reading / Resources Critical Thinking

Priority Assessments

1
2
3

Priority Labs & Diagnostics

1
2
3

Priority Nursing Interventions

1
2
3

Priority Medications

1

2

3

Priority Potential & Actual Complications

1

2

3

Priority Collaborative Goals

1

2

3

NurseThink Quick

CARE ACCORDING TO THE NCLEX® TEST PLAN

Safe and Effective Care: Management of Care, Coordinated Care, Safety and Infection Control

Health Promotion and Maintenance

Psychosocial Integrity

Physiological Integrity: Basic Care and Comfort, Pharmacological and Parenteral Therapies, Reduction of Risk Potential, and Physiological Adaptation

CARE ACCORDING TO QUALITY AND SAFETY STANDARDS

Patient-Centered Care

Teamwork and Collaboration

Evidence-Based Practice

Quality Improvement

Safety

Informatics

Buddy Review: _____   Faculty Review: _____

Grade Tracker

Related Exemplars

Related Concepts

Classroom Critical Thinking

Reading / Resources Critical Thinking

Priority Assessments

1
2
3

Priority Labs & Diagnostics

1
2
3

Priority Nursing Interventions

1
2
3

Priority Medications

1
2
3

Priority Potential & Actual Complications

1
2
3

Priority Collaborative Goals

1
2
3

NurseThink Notes

NurseThink Quick

CARE ACCORDING TO THE NCLEX® TEST PLAN

Safe and Effective Care: Management of Care, Coordinated Care, Safety and Infection Control

Health Promotion and Maintenance

Psychosocial Integrity

Physiological Integrity: Basic Care and Comfort, Pharmacological and Parenteral Therapies, Reduction of Risk Potential, and Physiological Adaptation

---

CARE ACCORDING TO QUALITY AND SAFETY STANDARDS

Patient-Centered Care

Teamwork and Collaboration

Evidence-Based Practice

Quality Improvement

Safety

Informatics

Buddy Review: _____   Faculty Review: _____

Grade Tracker

Related Exemplars

Related Concepts

Classroom Critical Thinking

Reading / Resources Critical Thinking

Priority Assessments

1
2
3

Priority Labs & Diagnostics

1
2
3

Priority Nursing Interventions

1
2
3

Priority Medications

1
2
3

Priority Potential & Actual Complications

1
2
3

Priority Collaborative Goals

1
2
3

NurseThink Quick

CARE ACCORDING TO THE NCLEX® TEST PLAN

Safe and Effective Care: Management of Care, Coordinated Care, Safety and Infection Control

Health Promotion and Maintenance

Psychosocial Integrity

Physiological Integrity: Basic Care and Comfort, Pharmacological and Parenteral Therapies, Reduction of Risk Potential, and Physiological Adaptation

CARE ACCORDING TO QUALITY AND SAFETY STANDARDS

Patient-Centered Care

Teamwork and Collaboration

Evidence-Based Practice

Quality Improvement

Safety

Informatics

Buddy Review: _____   Faculty Review: _____

Grade Tracker

Related Exemplars

Related Concepts

Classroom Critical Thinking

Reading / Resources Critical Thinking

Priority Assessments

1

2

3

Priority Labs & Diagnostics

1

2

3

Priority Nursing Interventions

1

2

3

Priority Medications

1

2

3

Priority Potential & Actual Complications

1

2

3

Priority Collaborative Goals

1

2

3

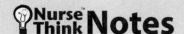
NurseThink Quick

Hypercalcemia: Signs and Symptoms	Hypercalcemia: Causes	Hypocalcemia: Signs and Symptoms
Groans, Moans, Bones, Stones, and Overtones **Groans:** constipation **Moans:** pain - joint aches **Bones:** loss of calcium from bones, bone metastasis **Stones:** kidney stones **Overtones:** psychiatric overtones - depression, confusion	***MD Pimps Me*** **M**alignancy **D**iuretics **P**arathyroid **I**mmobilization/ Idiopathic **M**ega doses of vitamins A, D P – Paget's Disease **S**arcoidosis **M**ilk alkali syndrome **E**ndocrine (Addison's disease, thyrotoxicosis)	***Cats*** **C**onvulsions **A**rrhythmias **T**etany **S**pasms and stridor

CARE ACCORDING TO THE NCLEX® TEST PLAN

Safe and Effective Care: Management of Care, Coordinated Care, Safety and Infection Control

Health Promotion and Maintenance

Psychosocial Integrity

Physiological Integrity: Basic Care and Comfort, Pharmacological and Parenteral Therapies, Reduction of Risk Potential, and Physiological Adaptation

CARE ACCORDING TO QUALITY AND SAFETY STANDARDS

Patient-Centered Care

Teamwork and Collaboration

Evidence-Based Practice

Quality Improvement

Safety

Informatics

Buddy Review: _____   Faculty Review: _____

Grade Tracker

Related Exemplars	**Related Concepts**

Classroom Critical Thinking	**Reading / Resources Critical Thinking**

Priority Assessments

1

2

3

Priority Labs & Diagnostics

1

2

3

Priority Nursing Interventions

1

2

3

Priority Medications

1

2

3

Priority Potential & Actual Complications

1

2

3

Priority Collaborative Goals

1

2

3

NurseThink Quick

Hyperkalemia: Causes
Machine
Medications - ACE inhibitors, NSAIDS
Acidosis - metabolic and respiratory
Cellular destruction - burns, traumatic injury
Hypoaldosteronism, hemolysis
Intake - excessive
Nephrons, renal failure
Excretion – impaired

Hyperkalemia: Signs and Symptoms
Murder
Muscle weakness
Urine, oliguria, anuria
Respiratory distress
Decreased cardiac contractility
ECG changes
Reflexes, hyperreflexia, or areflexia (flaccid)

Hyperkalemia: Treatment
Kind
Kayexalate
Insulin
Na HCO3
Diuretics

Hypokalemia: Signs and Symptoms
6 L's
Lethargy
Leg cramps
Limp muscles
Low, shallow respirations
Lethal cardiac dysrhythmias
Lots of urine (polyuria)

CARE ACCORDING TO THE NCLEX® TEST PLAN

Safe and Effective Care: Management of Care, Coordinated Care, Safety and Infection Control

Health Promotion and Maintenance

Psychosocial Integrity

Physiological Integrity: Basic Care and Comfort, Pharmacological and Parenteral Therapies, Reduction of Risk Potential, and Physiological Adaptation

CARE ACCORDING TO QUALITY AND SAFETY STANDARDS

Patient-Centered Care

Teamwork and Collaboration

Evidence-Based Practice

Quality Improvement

Safety

Informatics

Buddy Review: _____   Faculty Review: _____

Grade Tracker

Related Exemplars	Related Concepts

Classroom Critical Thinking	Reading / Resources Critical Thinking

Priority Assessments

1

2

3

Priority Labs & Diagnostics

1

2

3

Priority Nursing Interventions

1

2

3

Priority Medications

1

2

3

Priority Potential & Actual Complications

1

2

3

Priority Collaborative Goals

1

2

3

NurseThink Quick

CARE ACCORDING TO THE NCLEX® TEST PLAN

Safe and Effective Care: Management of Care, Coordinated Care, Safety and Infection Control

Health Promotion and Maintenance

Psychosocial Integrity

Physiological Integrity: Basic Care and Comfort, Pharmacological and Parenteral Therapies, Reduction of Risk Potential, and Physiological Adaptation

CARE ACCORDING TO QUALITY AND SAFETY STANDARDS

Patient-Centered Care

Teamwork and Collaboration

Evidence-Based Practice

Quality Improvement

Safety

Informatics

Buddy Review: _____   Faculty Review: _____

Grade Tracker

Related Exemplars	Related Concepts

Classroom Critical Thinking	Reading / Resources Critical Thinking

Priority Assessments

1

2

3

Priority Labs & Diagnostics

1

2

3

Priority Nursing Interventions

1

2

3

Priority Medications

1

2

3

Priority Potential & Actual Complications

1

2

3

Priority Collaborative Goals

1

2

3

NurseThink Quick

Hypernatremia: Causes
Model
Medications, meals
Osmotic diuretics
Diabetes insipidus
Excessive water loss
Low water intake

Hypernatremia: Signs and Symptoms
Fried
Fever (low grade), flushed skin
Restless and irritable
Increased fluid retention and increased BP
Edema (peripheral and pitting)
Decreased urinary output, dry mouth

Hyponatremia: Signs and Symptoms
Salt Loss
Stupor and coma
Anorexia, N&V
Lethargy
Tendon reflexes decreased
Limp muscles (weakness)
Orthostatic hypotension
Seizures and headaches
Stomach cramping

CARE ACCORDING TO THE NCLEX® TEST PLAN

Safe and Effective Care: Management of Care, Coordinated Care, Safety and Infection Control

Health Promotion and Maintenance

Psychosocial Integrity

Physiological Integrity: Basic Care and Comfort, Pharmacological and Parenteral Therapies, Reduction of Risk Potential, and Physiological Adaptation

CARE ACCORDING TO QUALITY AND SAFETY STANDARDS

Patient-Centered Care

Teamwork and Collaboration

Evidence-Based Practice

Quality Improvement

Safety

Informatics

Buddy Review: _____   Faculty Review: _____

Grade Tracker

Related Exemplars

Related Concepts

Classroom Critical Thinking

Reading / Resources Critical Thinking

Priority Assessments

1
2
3

Priority Labs & Diagnostics

1
2
3

Priority Nursing Interventions

1
2
3

Priority Medications

1
2
3

Priority Potential & Actual Complications

1
2
3

Priority Collaborative Goals

1
2
3

NurseThink Quick

CARE ACCORDING TO THE NCLEX® TEST PLAN

Safe and Effective Care: Management of Care, Coordinated Care, Safety and Infection Control

Health Promotion and Maintenance

Psychosocial Integrity

Physiological Integrity: Basic Care and Comfort, Pharmacological and Parenteral Therapies, Reduction of Risk Potential, and Physiological Adaptation

CARE ACCORDING TO QUALITY AND SAFETY STANDARDS

Patient-Centered Care

Teamwork and Collaboration

Evidence-Based Practice

Quality Improvement

Safety

Informatics

Buddy Review: _____   Faculty Review: _____

Grade Tracker

Related Exemplars

Related Concepts

Classroom Critical Thinking

Reading / Resources Critical Thinking

Priority Assessments
1
2
3

Priority Labs & Diagnostics
1
2
3

Priority Nursing Interventions
1
2
3

Priority Medications
1
2
3

Priority Potential & Actual Complications
1
2
3

Priority Collaborative Goals
1
2
3

CARE ACCORDING TO THE NCLEX® TEST PLAN

Safe and Effective Care: Management of Care, Coordinated Care, Safety and Infection Control

Health Promotion and Maintenance

Psychosocial Integrity

Physiological Integrity: Basic Care and Comfort, Pharmacological and Parenteral Therapies, Reduction of Risk Potential, and Physiological Adaptation

CARE ACCORDING TO QUALITY AND SAFETY STANDARDS

Patient-Centered Care

Teamwork and Collaboration

Evidence-Based Practice

Quality Improvement

Safety

Informatics

Buddy Review: _____   Faculty Review: _____

Grade Tracker

Related Exemplars	Related Concepts

Classroom Critical Thinking	Reading / Resources Critical Thinking

Priority Assessments

1

2

3

Priority Labs & Diagnostics

1

2

3

Priority Nursing Interventions

1

2

3

Priority Medications

1

2

3

Priority Potential & Actual Complications

1

2

3

Priority Collaborative Goals

1

2

3

NurseThink Quick

CARE ACCORDING TO THE NCLEX® TEST PLAN

Safe and Effective Care: Management of Care, Coordinated Care, Safety and Infection Control

Health Promotion and Maintenance

Psychosocial Integrity

Physiological Integrity: Basic Care and Comfort, Pharmacological and Parenteral Therapies, Reduction of Risk Potential, and Physiological Adaptation

CARE ACCORDING TO QUALITY AND SAFETY STANDARDS

Patient-Centered Care

Teamwork and Collaboration

Evidence-Based Practice

Quality Improvement

Safety

Informatics

Buddy Review: _____   Faculty Review: _____

Grade Tracker

Related Exemplars

Related Concepts

Classroom Critical Thinking

Reading / Resources Critical Thinking

Priority Assessments

1
2
3

Priority Labs & Diagnostics

1
2
3

Priority Nursing Interventions

1
2
3

Priority Medications

1
2
3

Priority Potential & Actual Complications

1
2
3

Priority Collaborative Goals

1
2
3

NurseThink Quick

Assistive devices: Canes
Coal
Cane
Opposite
Affected
Leg

CARE ACCORDING TO THE NCLEX® TEST PLAN

Safe and Effective Care: Management of Care, Coordinated Care, Safety and Infection Control

Health Promotion and Maintenance

Psychosocial Integrity

Physiological Integrity: Basic Care and Comfort, Pharmacological and Parenteral Therapies, Reduction of Risk Potential, and Physiological Adaptation

CARE ACCORDING TO QUALITY AND SAFETY STANDARDS

Patient-Centered Care

Teamwork and Collaboration

Evidence-Based Practice

Quality Improvement

Safety

Informatics

Buddy Review: _____   Faculty Review: _____

Grade Tracker

Related Exemplars	Related Concepts

Classroom Critical Thinking	Reading / Resources Critical Thinking

Priority Assessments

1
2
3

Priority Labs & Diagnostics

1
2
3

Priority Nursing Interventions

1
2
3

Priority Medications

1

2

3

Priority Potential & Actual Complications

1

2

3

Priority Collaborative Goals

1

2

3

NurseThink Quick

CARE ACCORDING TO THE NCLEX® TEST PLAN

Safe and Effective Care: Management of Care, Coordinated Care, Safety and Infection Control

Health Promotion and Maintenance

Psychosocial Integrity

Physiological Integrity: Basic Care and Comfort, Pharmacological and Parenteral Therapies, Reduction of Risk Potential, and Physiological Adaptation

CARE ACCORDING TO QUALITY AND SAFETY STANDARDS

Patient-Centered Care

Teamwork and Collaboration

Evidence-Based Practice

Quality Improvement

Safety

Informatics

Buddy Review: _____   Faculty Review: _____

Grade Tracker

Related Exemplars	Related Concepts

Classroom Critical Thinking	Reading / Resources Critical Thinking

Priority Assessments	Priority Labs & Diagnostics	Priority Nursing Interventions
1	1	1
2	2	2
3	3	3

Priority Medications	Priority Potential & Actual Complications	Priority Collaborative Goals
1	1	1
2	2	2
3	3	3

NurseThink Quick

Carpal Tunnel Syndrome	Carpal Tunnel Treatment	
Dog Arm Pit	***Wrist***	
Dialysis	**W**ear splints at night	
Obesity	**R**est	
Gout	**I**nject steroid	
Amyloid/Acromegaly	**S**urgical decompression	
Rheumatoid arthritis	**T**ake diuretics	
Myxedema		
Pregnancy		
Idiopathic		
Trauma		

CARE ACCORDING TO THE NCLEX® TEST PLAN

Safe and Effective Care: Management of Care, Coordinated Care, Safety and Infection Control

Health Promotion and Maintenance

Psychosocial Integrity

Physiological Integrity: Basic Care and Comfort, Pharmacological and Parenteral Therapies, Reduction of Risk Potential, and Physiological Adaptation

CARE ACCORDING TO QUALITY AND SAFETY STANDARDS

Patient-Centered Care

Teamwork and Collaboration

Evidence-Based Practice

Quality Improvement

Safety

Informatics

Buddy Review: _____   Faculty Review: _____

Grade Tracker

Related Exemplars	Related Concepts

Classroom Critical Thinking	Reading / Resources Critical Thinking

Priority Assessments

1
2
3

Priority Labs & Diagnostics

1
2
3

Priority Nursing Interventions

1
2
3

Priority Medications

1

2

3

Priority Potential & Actual Complications

1

2

3

Priority Collaborative Goals

1

2

3

 **Notes**

NurseThink Quick

Fracture: Description	**Fractures: Types**	**Fracture: Description**
Doctor	*Go C3PO*	*BLT Lard*
Displaced vs. non-displaced	**G**reenstick	**B**one
Open vs. closed	**O**pen	**L**ocation on bone
Complete vs. incomplete	**C**omplete/Closed/Comminuted	**T**ype of fracture
Transverse vs. linear	**P**artial	**L**engthening
Open	**O**thers	**A**ngulation
Reduction vs. closed reduction		**R**otation
		Displacement

Fractures: Management

Friar
First Aid
Reduction
Immobilization
Active
Rehabilitation

CARE ACCORDING TO THE NCLEX® TEST PLAN

Safe and Effective Care: Management of Care, Coordinated Care, Safety and Infection Control

Health Promotion and Maintenance

Psychosocial Integrity

Physiological Integrity: Basic Care and Comfort, Pharmacological and Parenteral Therapies, Reduction of Risk Potential, and Physiological Adaptation

CARE ACCORDING TO QUALITY AND SAFETY STANDARDS

Patient-Centered Care

Teamwork and Collaboration

Evidence-Based Practice

Quality Improvement

Safety

Informatics

Buddy Review: _____   Faculty Review: _____

Grade Tracker

Related Exemplars	Related Concepts

Classroom Critical Thinking	Reading / Resources Critical Thinking

Priority Assessments	Priority Labs & Diagnostics	Priority Nursing Interventions
1	1	1
2	2	2
3	3	3

Priority Medications	Priority Potential & Actual Complications	Priority Collaborative Goals
1	1	1
2	2	2
3	3	3

NurseThink Quick

CARE ACCORDING TO THE NCLEX® TEST PLAN

Safe and Effective Care: Management of Care, Coordinated Care, Safety and Infection Control

Health Promotion and Maintenance

Psychosocial Integrity

Physiological Integrity: Basic Care and Comfort, Pharmacological and Parenteral Therapies, Reduction of Risk Potential, and Physiological Adaptation

CARE ACCORDING TO QUALITY AND SAFETY STANDARDS

Patient-Centered Care

Teamwork and Collaboration

Evidence-Based Practice

Quality Improvement

Safety

Informatics

Buddy Review: _____   Faculty Review: _____

Grade Tracker

Related Exemplars	Related Concepts

Classroom Critical Thinking	Reading / Resources Critical Thinking

Priority Assessments	Priority Labs & Diagnostics	Priority Nursing Interventions
1	1	1
2	2	2
3	3	3

Priority Medications	Priority Potential & Actual Complications	Priority Collaborative Goals
1	1	1
2	2	2
3	3	3

NurseThink Notes

NurseThink Quick

<table>
<tr><td></td><td></td><td></td></tr>
</table>

CARE ACCORDING TO THE NCLEX® TEST PLAN

Safe and Effective Care: Management of Care, Coordinated Care, Safety and Infection Control

Health Promotion and Maintenance

Psychosocial Integrity

Physiological Integrity: Basic Care and Comfort, Pharmacological and Parenteral Therapies, Reduction of Risk Potential, and Physiological Adaptation

CARE ACCORDING TO QUALITY AND SAFETY STANDARDS

Patient-Centered Care

Teamwork and Collaboration

Evidence-Based Practice

Quality Improvement

Safety

Informatics

Buddy Review: _____   Faculty Review: _____

Grade Tracker

<table>
<tr><td></td><td></td><td></td><td></td><td></td><td></td><td></td><td></td><td></td><td></td><td></td><td></td><td></td><td></td><td></td><td></td><td></td><td></td></tr>
</table>

Related Exemplars

Related Concepts

Classroom Critical Thinking

Reading / Resources Critical Thinking

Priority Assessments

1
2
3

Priority Labs & Diagnostics

1
2
3

Priority Nursing Interventions

1
2
3

Priority Medications

1
2
3

Priority Potential & Actual Complications

1
2
3

Priority Collaborative Goals

1
2
3

NurseThink Quick

Restless Leg Syndrome: Symptoms
Urge
Urge or sensation to move the legs
Rest or stillness of the legs worsens the
    urge to move
Going is good
Evening or nighttime worsening of symp-
    toms		

CARE ACCORDING TO THE NCLEX® TEST PLAN

Safe and Effective Care: Management of Care, Coordinated Care, Safety and Infection Control

Health Promotion and Maintenance

Psychosocial Integrity

Physiological Integrity: Basic Care and Comfort, Pharmacological and Parenteral Therapies, Reduction of Risk Potential, and Physiological Adaptation

CARE ACCORDING TO QUALITY AND SAFETY STANDARDS

Patient-Centered Care

Teamwork and Collaboration

Evidence-Based Practice

Quality Improvement

Safety

Informatics

Buddy Review: _____   Faculty Review: _____

Grade Tracker

Related Exemplars	Related Concepts

Classroom Critical Thinking	Reading / Resources Critical Thinking

Priority Assessments

1
2
3

Priority Labs & Diagnostics

1
2
3

Priority Nursing Interventions

1
2
3

Priority Medications

1

2

3

Priority Potential & Actual Complications

1

2

3

Priority Collaborative Goals

1

2

3

NurseThink Quick

ALS: Symptoms		
ALS **A**nterior horn neuron loss **L**ower motor dominant effects **S**pino-cortical tract		

CARE ACCORDING TO THE NCLEX® TEST PLAN

Safe and Effective Care: Management of Care, Coordinated Care, Safety and Infection Control

Health Promotion and Maintenance

Psychosocial Integrity

Physiological Integrity: Basic Care and Comfort, Pharmacological and Parenteral Therapies, Reduction of Risk Potential, and Physiological Adaptation

CARE ACCORDING TO QUALITY AND SAFETY STANDARDS

Patient-Centered Care

Teamwork and Collaboration

Evidence-Based Practice

Quality Improvement

Safety

Informatics

Buddy Review: _____   Faculty Review: _____

Grade Tracker

Related Exemplars

Related Concepts

Classroom Critical Thinking

Reading / Resources Critical Thinking

Priority Assessments

1
2
3

Priority Labs & Diagnostics

1
2
3

Priority Nursing Interventions

1
2
3

Priority Medications

1
2
3

Priority Potential & Actual Complications

1
2
3

Priority Collaborative Goals

1
2
3

NurseThink Quick

CARE ACCORDING TO THE NCLEX® TEST PLAN

Safe and Effective Care: Management of Care, Coordinated Care, Safety and Infection Control

Health Promotion and Maintenance

Psychosocial Integrity

Physiological Integrity: Basic Care and Comfort, Pharmacological and Parenteral Therapies, Reduction of Risk Potential, and Physiological Adaptation

CARE ACCORDING TO QUALITY AND SAFETY STANDARDS

Patient-Centered Care

Teamwork and Collaboration

Evidence-Based Practice

Quality Improvement

Safety

Informatics

Buddy Review: _____   Faculty Review: _____

Grade Tracker

Related Exemplars

Related Concepts

Classroom Critical Thinking

Reading / Resources Critical Thinking

Priority Assessments

1

2

3

Priority Labs & Diagnostics

1

2

3

Priority Nursing Interventions

1

2

3

Priority Medications

1

2

3

Priority Potential & Actual Complications

1

2

3

Priority Collaborative Goals

1

2

3

NurseThink Quick

CARE ACCORDING TO THE NCLEX® TEST PLAN

Safe and Effective Care: Management of Care, Coordinated Care, Safety and Infection Control

Health Promotion and Maintenance

Psychosocial Integrity

Physiological Integrity: Basic Care and Comfort, Pharmacological and Parenteral Therapies, Reduction of Risk Potential, and Physiological Adaptation

CARE ACCORDING TO QUALITY AND SAFETY STANDARDS

Patient-Centered Care

Teamwork and Collaboration

Evidence-Based Practice

Quality Improvement

Safety

Informatics

Buddy Review: _____   Faculty Review: _____

Grade Tracker

Related Exemplars	Related Concepts

Classroom Critical Thinking	Reading / Resources Critical Thinking

Priority Assessments

1
2
3

Priority Labs & Diagnostics

1
2
3

Priority Nursing Interventions

1
2
3

Priority Medications

1

2

3

Priority Potential & Actual Complications

1

2

3

Priority Collaborative Goals

1

2

3

CARE ACCORDING TO THE NCLEX® TEST PLAN

Safe and Effective Care: Management of Care, Coordinated Care, Safety and Infection Control

Health Promotion and Maintenance

Psychosocial Integrity

Physiological Integrity: Basic Care and Comfort, Pharmacological and Parenteral Therapies, Reduction of Risk Potential, and Physiological Adaptation

CARE ACCORDING TO QUALITY AND SAFETY STANDARDS

Patient-Centered Care

Teamwork and Collaboration

Evidence-Based Practice

Quality Improvement

Safety

Informatics

Buddy Review: _____   Faculty Review: _____

Grade Tracker

Related Exemplars

Related Concepts

Classroom Critical Thinking

Reading / Resources Critical Thinking

Priority Assessments
1
2
3

Priority Labs & Diagnostics
1
2
3

Priority Nursing Interventions
1
2
3

Priority Medications
1
2
3

Priority Potential & Actual Complications
1
2
3

Priority Collaborative Goals
1
2
3

 **Notes**

NurseThink Quick

Multiple Sclerosis: Symptoms	Multiple Sclerosis: Patho	
Insular	MS attacks the Myelin Sheath, resulting in plaques.	
Intention tremor		
Nystagmus		
Slurred speech		
Uthoff's phenomenon		
Lhermitte's sign		
Ataxia		
Rebound		

CARE ACCORDING TO THE NCLEX® TEST PLAN

Safe and Effective Care: Management of Care, Coordinated Care, Safety and Infection Control

Health Promotion and Maintenance

Psychosocial Integrity

Physiological Integrity: Basic Care and Comfort, Pharmacological and Parenteral Therapies, Reduction of Risk Potential, and Physiological Adaptation

CARE ACCORDING TO QUALITY AND SAFETY STANDARDS

Patient-Centered Care

Teamwork and Collaboration

Evidence-Based Practice

Quality Improvement

Safety

Informatics

Buddy Review: _____   Faculty Review: _____

Grade Tracker

Related Exemplars	Related Concepts

Classroom Critical Thinking	Reading / Resources Critical Thinking

Priority Assessments

1
2
3

Priority Labs & Diagnostics

1
2
3

Priority Nursing Interventions

1
2
3

Priority Medications

1
2
3

Priority Potential & Actual Complications

1
2
3

Priority Collaborative Goals

1
2
3

NurseThink Quick

CARE ACCORDING TO THE NCLEX® TEST PLAN

Safe and Effective Care: Management of Care, Coordinated Care, Safety and Infection Control

Health Promotion and Maintenance

Psychosocial Integrity

Physiological Integrity: Basic Care and Comfort, Pharmacological and Parenteral Therapies, Reduction of Risk Potential, and Physiological Adaptation

CARE ACCORDING TO QUALITY AND SAFETY STANDARDS

Patient-Centered Care

Teamwork and Collaboration

Evidence-Based Practice

Quality Improvement

Safety

Informatics

Buddy Review: _____   Faculty Review: _____

Grade Tracker

Related Exemplars	Related Concepts

Classroom Critical Thinking	Reading / Resources Critical Thinking

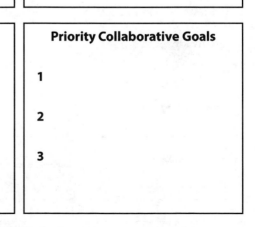

Priority Assessments
1
2
3

Priority Labs & Diagnostics
1
2
3

Priority Nursing Interventions
1
2
3

Priority Medications
1
2
3

Priority Potential & Actual Complications
1
2
3

Priority Collaborative Goals
1
2
3

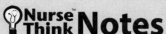 **Nurse Think Notes**

NurseThink Quick

Parkinson's Medications	**Parkinson's Symptoms**	
Ali Loves Boxing Matches	***Parkinson's***	
Amantadine	**P**ill rolling	
Levodopa	**A**kinesis	
Bromocriptine	**R**igidity	
MAO inhibitors	**K**yphosis	
	Instability	
	Neck titubation	
	Shuffling gait	
	Oculogyric crisis	
	Nose tab (glabellar)	
	Small writing	

CARE ACCORDING TO THE NCLEX® TEST PLAN

Safe and Effective Care: Management of Care, Coordinated Care, Safety and Infection Control

Health Promotion and Maintenance

Psychosocial Integrity

Physiological Integrity: Basic Care and Comfort, Pharmacological and Parenteral Therapies, Reduction of Risk Potential, and Physiological Adaptation

CARE ACCORDING TO QUALITY AND SAFETY STANDARDS

Patient-Centered Care

Teamwork and Collaboration

Evidence-Based Practice

Quality Improvement

Safety

Informatics

Buddy Review: _____   Faculty Review: _____

Grade Tracker

Related Exemplars

Related Concepts

Classroom Critical Thinking

Reading / Resources Critical Thinking

Priority Assessments
1
2
3

Priority Labs & Diagnostics
1
2
3

Priority Nursing Interventions
1
2
3

Priority Medications
1
2
3

Priority Potential & Actual Complications
1
2
3

Priority Collaborative Goals
1
2
3

NurseThink Notes

NurseThink Quick

CARE ACCORDING TO THE NCLEX® TEST PLAN

Safe and Effective Care: Management of Care, Coordinated Care, Safety and Infection Control

Health Promotion and Maintenance

Psychosocial Integrity

Physiological Integrity: Basic Care and Comfort, Pharmacological and Parenteral Therapies, Reduction of Risk Potential, and Physiological Adaptation

CARE ACCORDING TO QUALITY AND SAFETY STANDARDS

Patient-Centered Care

Teamwork and Collaboration

Evidence-Based Practice

Quality Improvement

Safety

Informatics

Buddy Review: _____ Faculty Review: _____

Grade Tracker

Related Exemplars	**Related Concepts**

Classroom Critical Thinking	**Reading / Resources Critical Thinking**

Priority Assessments

1

2

3

Priority Labs & Diagnostics

1

2

3

Priority Nursing Interventions

1

2

3

Priority Medications

1

2

3

Priority Potential & Actual Complications

1

2

3

Priority Collaborative Goals

1

2

3

NurseThink Quick

Seizure: Quick History Taking		
Fact **F**ocus: generalized vs. local activity **A**ctivity: tonic clonic vs. absence **C**olor: red, blue, ashen **T**ime: length of seizure		

CARE ACCORDING TO THE NCLEX® TEST PLAN

Safe and Effective Care: Management of Care, Coordinated Care, Safety and Infection Control

Health Promotion and Maintenance

Psychosocial Integrity

Physiological Integrity: Basic Care and Comfort, Pharmacological and Parenteral Therapies, Reduction of Risk Potential, and Physiological Adaptation

CARE ACCORDING TO QUALITY AND SAFETY STANDARDS

Patient-Centered Care

Teamwork and Collaboration

Evidence-Based Practice

Quality Improvement

Safety

Informatics

Buddy Review: _____   Faculty Review: _____

Grade Tracker

Related Exemplars

Related Concepts

Classroom Critical Thinking

Reading / Resources Critical Thinking

Priority Assessments

1

2

3

Priority Labs & Diagnostics

1

2

3

Priority Nursing Interventions

1

2

3

Priority Medications

1

2

3

Priority Potential & Actual Complications

1

2

3

Priority Collaborative Goals

1

2

3

NurseThink Quick

CARE ACCORDING TO THE NCLEX® TEST PLAN

Safe and Effective Care: Management of Care, Coordinated Care, Safety and Infection Control

Health Promotion and Maintenance

Psychosocial Integrity

Physiological Integrity: Basic Care and Comfort, Pharmacological and Parenteral Therapies, Reduction of Risk Potential, and Physiological Adaptation

CARE ACCORDING TO QUALITY AND SAFETY STANDARDS

Patient-Centered Care

Teamwork and Collaboration

Evidence-Based Practice

Quality Improvement

Safety

Informatics

Buddy Review: _____   Faculty Review: _____

Grade Tracker

Related Exemplars	Related Concepts

Classroom Critical Thinking	Reading / Resources Critical Thinking

Priority Assessments

1

2

3

Priority Labs & Diagnostics

1

2

3

Priority Nursing Interventions

1

2

3

Priority Medications

1

2

3

Priority Potential & Actual Complications

1

2

3

Priority Collaborative Goals

1

2

3

NurseThink Quick

CARE ACCORDING TO THE NCLEX® TEST PLAN

Safe and Effective Care: Management of Care, Coordinated Care, Safety and Infection Control

Health Promotion and Maintenance

Psychosocial Integrity

Physiological Integrity: Basic Care and Comfort, Pharmacological and Parenteral Therapies, Reduction of Risk Potential, and Physiological Adaptation

CARE ACCORDING TO QUALITY AND SAFETY STANDARDS

Patient-Centered Care

Teamwork and Collaboration

Evidence-Based Practice

Quality Improvement

Safety

Informatics

Buddy Review: _____   Faculty Review: _____

Grade Tracker

Related Exemplars	Related Concepts

Classroom Critical Thinking	Reading / Resources Critical Thinking

Priority Assessments	Priority Labs & Diagnostics	Priority Nursing Interventions
1	1	1
2	2	2
3	3	3

Priority Medications	Priority Potential & Actual Complications	Priority Collaborative Goals
1	1	1
2	2	2
3	3	3

NurseThink Quick

Cataracts: Differential

CATARAct
Congenital
Aging
Toxicity (Steroids, etc.)
Accidents
Radiation
Abnormal metabolism

CARE ACCORDING TO THE NCLEX® TEST PLAN

Safe and Effective Care: Management of Care, Coordinated Care, Safety and Infection Control

Health Promotion and Maintenance

Psychosocial Integrity

Physiological Integrity: Basic Care and Comfort, Pharmacological and Parenteral Therapies, Reduction of Risk Potential, and Physiological Adaptation

CARE ACCORDING TO QUALITY AND SAFETY STANDARDS

Patient-Centered Care

Teamwork and Collaboration

Evidence-Based Practice

Quality Improvement

Safety

Informatics

Buddy Review: _____   Faculty Review: _____

Grade Tracker

Related Exemplars	Related Concepts

Classroom Critical Thinking	Reading / Resources Critical Thinking

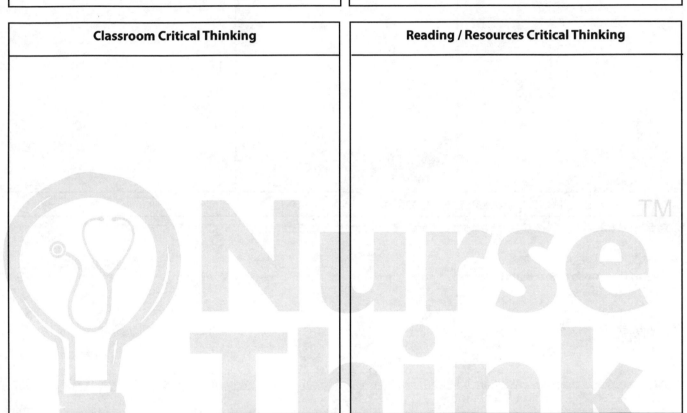

Priority Assessments	Priority Labs & Diagnostics	Priority Nursing Interventions
1	1	1
2	2	2
3	3	3

Priority Medications	Priority Potential & Actual Complications	Priority Collaborative Goals
1	1	1
2	2	2
3	3	3

NurseThink Quick

CARE ACCORDING TO THE NCLEX® TEST PLAN

Safe and Effective Care: Management of Care, Coordinated Care, Safety and Infection Control

Health Promotion and Maintenance

Psychosocial Integrity

Physiological Integrity: Basic Care and Comfort, Pharmacological and Parenteral Therapies, Reduction of Risk Potential, and Physiological Adaptation

CARE ACCORDING TO QUALITY AND SAFETY STANDARDS

Patient-Centered Care

Teamwork and Collaboration

Evidence-Based Practice

Quality Improvement

Safety

Informatics

Buddy Review: _____   Faculty Review: _____

Grade Tracker

 **Notes**

Related Exemplars	Related Concepts

Classroom Critical Thinking	Reading / Resources Critical Thinking

Priority Assessments
1
2
3

Priority Labs & Diagnostics
1
2
3

Priority Nursing Interventions
1
2
3

Priority Medications
1
2
3

Priority Potential & Actual Complications
1
2
3

Priority Collaborative Goals
1
2
3

NurseThink Quick

<table>
<tr><td></td><td></td><td></td></tr>
</table>

CARE ACCORDING TO THE NCLEX® TEST PLAN

Safe and Effective Care: Management of Care, Coordinated Care, Safety and Infection Control

Health Promotion and Maintenance

Psychosocial Integrity

Physiological Integrity: Basic Care and Comfort, Pharmacological and Parenteral Therapies, Reduction of Risk Potential, and Physiological Adaptation

CARE ACCORDING TO QUALITY AND SAFETY STANDARDS

Patient-Centered Care

Teamwork and Collaboration

Evidence-Based Practice

Quality Improvement

Safety

Informatics

Buddy Review: _____   Faculty Review: _____

Grade Tracker

Related Exemplars	**Related Concepts**

Classroom Critical Thinking	**Reading / Resources Critical Thinking**

Priority Assessments

1

2

3

Priority Labs & Diagnostics

1

2

3

Priority Nursing Interventions

1

2

3

Priority Medications

1

2

3

Priority Potential & Actual Complications

1

2

3

Priority Collaborative Goals

1

2

3

NurseThink Quick

CARE ACCORDING TO THE NCLEX® TEST PLAN

Safe and Effective Care: Management of Care, Coordinated Care, Safety and Infection Control

Health Promotion and Maintenance

Psychosocial Integrity

Physiological Integrity: Basic Care and Comfort, Pharmacological and Parenteral Therapies, Reduction of Risk Potential, and Physiological Adaptation

CARE ACCORDING TO QUALITY AND SAFETY STANDARDS

Patient-Centered Care

Teamwork and Collaboration

Evidence-Based Practice

Quality Improvement

Safety

Informatics

Buddy Review: _____   Faculty Review: _____

Grade Tracker

Related Exemplars	Related Concepts

Classroom Critical Thinking	Reading / Resources Critical Thinking

Priority Assessments	Priority Labs & Diagnostics	Priority Nursing Interventions
1	1	1
2	2	2
3	3	3

Priority Medications	Priority Potential & Actual Complications	Priority Collaborative Goals
1	1	1
2	2	2
3	3	3

NurseThink Quick

CARE ACCORDING TO THE NCLEX® TEST PLAN

Safe and Effective Care: Management of Care, Coordinated Care, Safety and Infection Control

Health Promotion and Maintenance

Psychosocial Integrity

Physiological Integrity: Basic Care and Comfort, Pharmacological and Parenteral Therapies, Reduction of Risk Potential, and Physiological Adaptation

CARE ACCORDING TO QUALITY AND SAFETY STANDARDS

Patient-Centered Care

Teamwork and Collaboration

Evidence-Based Practice

Quality Improvement

Safety

Informatics

Buddy Review: _____   Faculty Review: _____

Grade Tracker

Related Exemplars

Related Concepts

Classroom Critical Thinking

Reading / Resources Critical Thinking

Priority Assessments

1
2
3

Priority Labs & Diagnostics

1
2
3

Priority Nursing Interventions

1
2
3

Priority Medications

1
2
3

Priority Potential & Actual Complications

1
2
3

Priority Collaborative Goals

1
2
3

NurseThink Quick

CARE ACCORDING TO THE NCLEX® TEST PLAN

Safe and Effective Care: Management of Care, Coordinated Care, Safety and Infection Control

Health Promotion and Maintenance

Psychosocial Integrity

Physiological Integrity: Basic Care and Comfort, Pharmacological and Parenteral Therapies, Reduction of Risk Potential, and Physiological Adaptation

CARE ACCORDING TO QUALITY AND SAFETY STANDARDS

Patient-Centered Care

Teamwork and Collaboration

Evidence-Based Practice

Quality Improvement

Safety

Informatics

Buddy Review: _____   Faculty Review: _____

Grade Tracker

Related Exemplars

Related Concepts

Classroom Critical Thinking

Reading / Resources Critical Thinking

Priority Assessments

1
2
3

Priority Labs & Diagnostics

1
2
3

Priority Nursing Interventions

1
2
3

Priority Medications

1
2
3

Priority Potential & Actual Complications

1
2
3

Priority Collaborative Goals

1
2
3

NurseThink Quick

CARE ACCORDING TO THE NCLEX® TEST PLAN

Safe and Effective Care: Management of Care, Coordinated Care, Safety and Infection Control

Health Promotion and Maintenance

Psychosocial Integrity

Physiological Integrity: Basic Care and Comfort, Pharmacological and Parenteral Therapies, Reduction of Risk Potential, and Physiological Adaptation

CARE ACCORDING TO QUALITY AND SAFETY STANDARDS

Patient-Centered Care

Teamwork and Collaboration

Evidence-Based Practice

Quality Improvement

Safety

Informatics

Buddy Review: _____   Faculty Review: _____

Grade Tracker

Related Exemplars	Related Concepts

Classroom Critical Thinking	Reading / Resources Critical Thinking

Priority Assessments	Priority Labs & Diagnostics	Priority Nursing Interventions
1	1	1
2	2	2
3	3	3

Priority Medications	Priority Potential & Actual Complications	Priority Collaborative Goals
1	1	1
2	2	2
3	3	3

NurseThink Quick

CARE ACCORDING TO THE NCLEX® TEST PLAN

Safe and Effective Care: Management of Care, Coordinated Care, Safety and Infection Control

Health Promotion and Maintenance

Psychosocial Integrity

Physiological Integrity: Basic Care and Comfort, Pharmacological and Parenteral Therapies, Reduction of Risk Potential, and Physiological Adaptation

CARE ACCORDING TO QUALITY AND SAFETY STANDARDS

Patient-Centered Care

Teamwork and Collaboration

Evidence-Based Practice

Quality Improvement

Safety

Informatics

Buddy Review: _____   Faculty Review: _____

Grade Tracker

Related Exemplars

Related Concepts

Classroom Critical Thinking

Reading / Resources Critical Thinking

Priority Assessments

1

2

3

Priority Labs & Diagnostics

1

2

3

Priority Nursing Interventions

1

2

3

Priority Medications

1

2

3

Priority Potential & Actual Complications

1

2

3

Priority Collaborative Goals

1

2

3

 **Notes**

NurseThink Quick

Appendicitis: Assessment ***Pains*** **P**ain, RLQ **A**norexia **I**ncreased temperature **N**ausea **S**igns (McBurney's Psoas)		

CARE ACCORDING TO THE NCLEX® TEST PLAN

Safe and Effective Care: Management of Care, Coordinated Care, Safety and Infection Control

Health Promotion and Maintenance

Psychosocial Integrity

Physiological Integrity: Basic Care and Comfort, Pharmacological and Parenteral Therapies, Reduction of Risk Potential, and Physiological Adaptation

CARE ACCORDING TO QUALITY AND SAFETY STANDARDS

Patient-Centered Care

Teamwork and Collaboration

Evidence-Based Practice

Quality Improvement

Safety

Informatics

Buddy Review: _____   Faculty Review: _____

Grade Tracker

Related Exemplars	Related Concepts

Classroom Critical Thinking	Reading / Resources Critical Thinking

Priority Assessments	Priority Labs & Diagnostics	Priority Nursing Interventions
1	1	1
2	2	2
3	3	3

Priority Medications	Priority Potential & Actual Complications	Priority Collaborative Goals
1	1	1
2	2	2
3	3	3

NurseThink Quick

Cholelithiasis: Risk Factors	Charcot's Triad (gallstones)	
5 F's	**3 C's**	
Female	**C**olor change (jaundice)	
Fair skinned	**C**olic (biliary) pain	
Fat	**C**hills and fever	
Forty		
Fertile		

CARE ACCORDING TO THE NCLEX® TEST PLAN

Safe and Effective Care: Management of Care, Coordinated Care, Safety and Infection Control

Health Promotion and Maintenance

Psychosocial Integrity

Physiological Integrity: Basic Care and Comfort, Pharmacological and Parenteral Therapies, Reduction of Risk Potential, and Physiological Adaptation

CARE ACCORDING TO QUALITY AND SAFETY STANDARDS

Patient-Centered Care

Teamwork and Collaboration

Evidence-Based Practice

Quality Improvement

Safety

Informatics

Buddy Review: _____   Faculty Review: _____

Grade Tracker

Related Exemplars	Related Concepts

Classroom Critical Thinking	Reading / Resources Critical Thinking

Priority Assessments

1
2
3

Priority Labs & Diagnostics

1
2
3

Priority Nursing Interventions

1
2
3

Priority Medications

1
2
3

Priority Potential & Actual Complications

1
2
3

Priority Collaborative Goals

1
2
3

NurseThink Quick

CARE ACCORDING TO THE NCLEX® TEST PLAN

Safe and Effective Care: Management of Care, Coordinated Care, Safety and Infection Control

Health Promotion and Maintenance

Psychosocial Integrity

Physiological Integrity: Basic Care and Comfort, Pharmacological and Parenteral Therapies, Reduction of Risk Potential, and Physiological Adaptation

CARE ACCORDING TO QUALITY AND SAFETY STANDARDS

Patient-Centered Care

Teamwork and Collaboration

Evidence-Based Practice

Quality Improvement

Safety

Informatics

Buddy Review: _____   Faculty Review: _____

Grade Tracker

Related Exemplars

Related Concepts

Classroom Critical Thinking

Reading / Resources Critical Thinking

Priority Assessments

1
2
3

Priority Labs & Diagnostics

1
2
3

Priority Nursing Interventions

1
2
3

Priority Medications

1
2
3

Priority Potential & Actual Complications

1
2
3

Priority Collaborative Goals

1
2
3

NurseThink Notes

NurseThink Quick

CARE ACCORDING TO THE NCLEX® TEST PLAN

Safe and Effective Care: Management of Care, Coordinated Care, Safety and Infection Control

Health Promotion and Maintenance

Psychosocial Integrity

Physiological Integrity: Basic Care and Comfort, Pharmacological and Parenteral Therapies, Reduction of Risk Potential, and Physiological Adaptation

CARE ACCORDING TO QUALITY AND SAFETY STANDARDS

Patient-Centered Care

Teamwork and Collaboration

Evidence-Based Practice

Quality Improvement

Safety

Informatics

Buddy Review: _____ Faculty Review: _____

Grade Tracker

Related Exemplars

Related Concepts

Classroom Critical Thinking

Reading / Resources Critical Thinking

Priority Assessments

1
2
3

Priority Labs & Diagnostics

1
2
3

Priority Nursing Interventions

1
2
3

Priority Medications

1
2
3

Priority Potential & Actual Complications

1
2
3

Priority Collaborative Goals

1
2
3

NurseThink Notes

NurseThink Quick

CARE ACCORDING TO THE NCLEX® TEST PLAN

Safe and Effective Care: Management of Care, Coordinated Care, Safety and Infection Control

Health Promotion and Maintenance

Psychosocial Integrity

Physiological Integrity: Basic Care and Comfort, Pharmacological and Parenteral Therapies, Reduction of Risk Potential, and Physiological Adaptation

CARE ACCORDING TO QUALITY AND SAFETY STANDARDS

Patient-Centered Care

Teamwork and Collaboration

Evidence-Based Practice

Quality Improvement

Safety

Informatics

Buddy Review: _____   Faculty Review: _____

Grade Tracker

Related Exemplars	Related Concepts

Classroom Critical Thinking	Reading / Resources Critical Thinking

Priority Assessments

1

2

3

Priority Labs & Diagnostics

1

2

3

Priority Nursing Interventions

1

2

3

Priority Medications

1

2

3

Priority Potential & Actual Complications

1

2

3

Priority Collaborative Goals

1

2

3

NurseThink Quick

CARE ACCORDING TO THE NCLEX® TEST PLAN

Safe and Effective Care: Management of Care, Coordinated Care, Safety and Infection Control

Health Promotion and Maintenance

Psychosocial Integrity

Physiological Integrity: Basic Care and Comfort, Pharmacological and Parenteral Therapies, Reduction of Risk Potential, and Physiological Adaptation

CARE ACCORDING TO QUALITY AND SAFETY STANDARDS

Patient-Centered Care

Teamwork and Collaboration

Evidence-Based Practice

Quality Improvement

Safety

Informatics

Buddy Review: _____   Faculty Review: _____

Grade Tracker

Related Exemplars

Related Concepts

Classroom Critical Thinking

Reading / Resources Critical Thinking

Priority Assessments

1
2
3

Priority Labs & Diagnostics

1
2
3

Priority Nursing Interventions

1
2
3

Priority Medications

1
2
3

Priority Potential & Actual Complications

1
2
3

Priority Collaborative Goals

1
2
3

NurseThink Quick

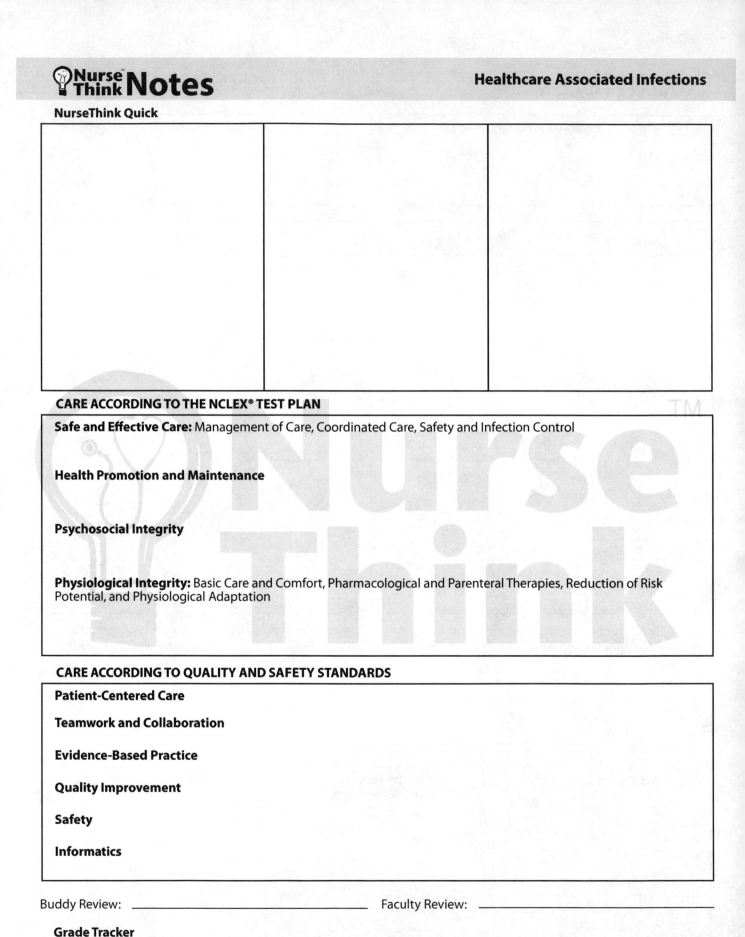

CARE ACCORDING TO THE NCLEX® TEST PLAN

Safe and Effective Care: Management of Care, Coordinated Care, Safety and Infection Control

Health Promotion and Maintenance

Psychosocial Integrity

Physiological Integrity: Basic Care and Comfort, Pharmacological and Parenteral Therapies, Reduction of Risk Potential, and Physiological Adaptation

CARE ACCORDING TO QUALITY AND SAFETY STANDARDS

Patient-Centered Care

Teamwork and Collaboration

Evidence-Based Practice

Quality Improvement

Safety

Informatics

Buddy Review: _____   Faculty Review: _____

Grade Tracker

Related Exemplars

Related Concepts

Classroom Critical Thinking

Reading / Resources Critical Thinking

Priority Assessments

1

2

3

Priority Labs & Diagnostics

1

2

3

Priority Nursing Interventions

1

2

3

Priority Medications

1

2

3

Priority Potential & Actual Complications

1

2

3

Priority Collaborative Goals

1

2

3

NurseThink Quick

CARE ACCORDING TO THE NCLEX® TEST PLAN

Safe and Effective Care: Management of Care, Coordinated Care, Safety and Infection Control

Health Promotion and Maintenance

Psychosocial Integrity

Physiological Integrity: Basic Care and Comfort, Pharmacological and Parenteral Therapies, Reduction of Risk Potential, and Physiological Adaptation

CARE ACCORDING TO QUALITY AND SAFETY STANDARDS

Patient-Centered Care

Teamwork and Collaboration

Evidence-Based Practice

Quality Improvement

Safety

Informatics

Buddy Review: _____ Faculty Review: _____

Grade Tracker

Related Exemplars	Related Concepts

Classroom Critical Thinking	Reading / Resources Critical Thinking

Priority Assessments	Priority Labs & Diagnostics	Priority Nursing Interventions
1	1	1
2	2	2
3	3	3

Priority Medications	Priority Potential & Actual Complications	Priority Collaborative Goals
1	1	1
2	2	2
3	3	3

NurseThink Quick

CARE ACCORDING TO THE NCLEX® TEST PLAN

Safe and Effective Care: Management of Care, Coordinated Care, Safety and Infection Control

Health Promotion and Maintenance

Psychosocial Integrity

Physiological Integrity: Basic Care and Comfort, Pharmacological and Parenteral Therapies, Reduction of Risk Potential, and Physiological Adaptation

CARE ACCORDING TO QUALITY AND SAFETY STANDARDS

Patient-Centered Care

Teamwork and Collaboration

Evidence-Based Practice

Quality Improvement

Safety

Informatics

Buddy Review: _____   Faculty Review: _____

Grade Tracker

Related Exemplars

Related Concepts

Classroom Critical Thinking

Reading / Resources Critical Thinking

Priority Assessments

1
2
3

Priority Labs & Diagnostics

1
2
3

Priority Nursing Interventions

1
2
3

Priority Medications

1
2
3

Priority Potential & Actual Complications

1
2
3

Priority Collaborative Goals

1
2
3

NurseThink Quick

Immunization Reaction: Signs and Symptoms		
Fisher Flag **F**ever **I**tching **S**tiffness **H**eadache **E**dema **R**edness **F**ussy **L**ocalized tenderness **A**ppetite decrease **G**eneral aches and pains		

CARE ACCORDING TO THE NCLEX® TEST PLAN

Safe and Effective Care: Management of Care, Coordinated Care, Safety and Infection Control

Health Promotion and Maintenance

Psychosocial Integrity

Physiological Integrity: Basic Care and Comfort, Pharmacological and Parenteral Therapies, Reduction of Risk Potential, and Physiological Adaptation

CARE ACCORDING TO QUALITY AND SAFETY STANDARDS

Patient-Centered Care

Teamwork and Collaboration

Evidence-Based Practice

Quality Improvement

Safety

Informatics

Buddy Review: _____   Faculty Review: _____

Grade Tracker

Related Exemplars

Related Concepts

Classroom Critical Thinking

Reading / Resources Critical Thinking

Priority Assessments

1

2

3

Priority Labs & Diagnostics

1

2

3

Priority Nursing Interventions

1

2

3

Priority Medications

1

2

3

Priority Potential & Actual Complications

1

2

3

Priority Collaborative Goals

1

2

3

NurseThink Quick

CARE ACCORDING TO THE NCLEX® TEST PLAN

Safe and Effective Care: Management of Care, Coordinated Care, Safety and Infection Control

Health Promotion and Maintenance

Psychosocial Integrity

Physiological Integrity: Basic Care and Comfort, Pharmacological and Parenteral Therapies, Reduction of Risk Potential, and Physiological Adaptation

CARE ACCORDING TO QUALITY AND SAFETY STANDARDS

Patient-Centered Care

Teamwork and Collaboration

Evidence-Based Practice

Quality Improvement

Safety

Informatics

Buddy Review: _____   Faculty Review: _____

Grade Tracker

Related Exemplars

Related Concepts

Classroom Critical Thinking

Reading / Resources Critical Thinking

Priority Assessments

1
2
3

Priority Labs & Diagnostics

1
2
3

Priority Nursing Interventions

1
2
3

Priority Medications

1
2
3

Priority Potential & Actual Complications

1
2
3

Priority Collaborative Goals

1
2
3

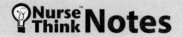
NurseThink Quick

AIDS Pathogens	HIV Infection: High-Risk Groups	AIDS Dementia Complex

AIDS Pathogens

The Major Pathogens Concerning Complete T-Cell Collapse

Toxoplasma gondii
M. avium intracellular
Pneumocystis carinii
Candida albicans
Cryptococcus neoformans
Tuberculosis
CMV
Cryptosporidium parvum

HIV Infection: High-Risk Groups

HHIV

Homosexuals
Hemophiliacs
IV drug abuses

AIDS Dementia Complex

AIDS

Atrophy of cortex
Infection/Inflammation
Demyelination
Six months death

CARE ACCORDING TO THE NCLEX® TEST PLAN

Safe and Effective Care: Management of Care, Coordinated Care, Safety and Infection Control

Health Promotion and Maintenance

Psychosocial Integrity

Physiological Integrity: Basic Care and Comfort, Pharmacological and Parenteral Therapies, Reduction of Risk Potential, and Physiological Adaptation

CARE ACCORDING TO QUALITY AND SAFETY STANDARDS

Patient-Centered Care

Teamwork and Collaboration

Evidence-Based Practice

Quality Improvement

Safety

Informatics

Buddy Review: _____   Faculty Review: _____

Grade Tracker

Related Exemplars	Related Concepts

Classroom Critical Thinking	Reading / Resources Critical Thinking

Priority Assessments

1

2

3

Priority Labs & Diagnostics

1

2

3

Priority Nursing Interventions

1

2

3

Priority Medications

1

2

3

Priority Potential & Actual Complications

1

2

3

Priority Collaborative Goals

1

2

3

 **Notes**

NurseThink Quick

SLE: Symptoms	**Lupus: Drug Inducing It**	**SLE: Factors Activating SLE**
Soap Brain MD	***Hip***	***UV Prism***
Serositis	**H**ydralazine	**UV** (sunshine)
Oral ulcers	**I**NH	**P**regnancy
Arthritis	**P**rocainamide	**R**educed drug (steroid)
Photosensitivity		**I**nfection
Blood disorder		**S**tress
Renal disorder		**M**ore drugs
Antinuclear antibody test positive		
Immunologic disorder		
Neurologic disorder		
Malar rash		
Discoid rash		

CARE ACCORDING TO THE NCLEX® TEST PLAN

Safe and Effective Care: Management of Care, Coordinated Care, Safety and Infection Control

Health Promotion and Maintenance

Psychosocial Integrity

Physiological Integrity: Basic Care and Comfort, Pharmacological and Parenteral Therapies, Reduction of Risk Potential, and Physiological Adaptation

CARE ACCORDING TO QUALITY AND SAFETY STANDARDS

Patient-Centered Care

Teamwork and Collaboration

Evidence-Based Practice

Quality Improvement

Safety

Informatics

Buddy Review: _____   Faculty Review: _____

Grade Tracker

Related Exemplars

Related Concepts

Classroom Critical Thinking

Reading / Resources Critical Thinking

Priority Assessments

1

2

3

Priority Labs & Diagnostics

1

2

3

Priority Nursing Interventions

1

2

3

Priority Medications

1

2

3

Priority Potential & Actual Complications

1

2

3

Priority Collaborative Goals

1

2

3

NurseThink Notes

NurseThink Quick

Rheumatoid Arthritis: Features		
Rheumatoid **R**agocytes/Rheumatoid factor **H**LA-DR4/Hla-Dw4 **E**SR increase/Extra-articular features **U**lnar deviation **M**orning stiffness **A**nkylosis/Atlantoaxial joint subluxation/ Autoimmune/ANA **T**-cells (CD4)/ **O**steopenia **I**nflammatory synovial tissue **D**eformities		

CARE ACCORDING TO THE NCLEX® TEST PLAN

Safe and Effective Care: Management of Care, Coordinated Care, Safety and Infection Control

Health Promotion and Maintenance

Psychosocial Integrity

Physiological Integrity: Basic Care and Comfort, Pharmacological and Parenteral Therapies, Reduction of Risk Potential, and Physiological Adaptation

CARE ACCORDING TO QUALITY AND SAFETY STANDARDS

Patient-Centered Care

Teamwork and Collaboration

Evidence-Based Practice

Quality Improvement

Safety

Informatics

Buddy Review: _____   Faculty Review: _____

Grade Tracker

 **Notes**

Cystitis

Related Exemplars

Related Concepts

Classroom Critical Thinking

Reading / Resources Critical Thinking

Priority Assessments
1
2
3

Priority Labs & Diagnostics
1
2
3

Priority Nursing Interventions
1
2
3

Priority Medications
1
2
3

Priority Potential & Actual Complications
1
2
3

Priority Collaborative Goals
1
2
3

CARE ACCORDING TO THE NCLEX® TEST PLAN

Safe and Effective Care: Management of Care, Coordinated Care, Safety and Infection Control

Health Promotion and Maintenance

Psychosocial Integrity

Physiological Integrity: Basic Care and Comfort, Pharmacological and Parenteral Therapies, Reduction of Risk Potential, and Physiological Adaptation

CARE ACCORDING TO QUALITY AND SAFETY STANDARDS

Patient-Centered Care

Teamwork and Collaboration

Evidence-Based Practice

Quality Improvement

Safety

Informatics

Buddy Review: _____   Faculty Review: _____

Grade Tracker

Related Exemplars	Related Concepts

Classroom Critical Thinking	Reading / Resources Critical Thinking

Priority Assessments	Priority Labs & Diagnostics	Priority Nursing Interventions
1	1	1
2	2	2
3	3	3

Priority Medications	Priority Potential & Actual Complications	Priority Collaborative Goals
1	1	1
2	2	2
3	3	3

NurseThink Quick

CARE ACCORDING TO THE NCLEX® TEST PLAN

Safe and Effective Care: Management of Care, Coordinated Care, Safety and Infection Control

Health Promotion and Maintenance

Psychosocial Integrity

Physiological Integrity: Basic Care and Comfort, Pharmacological and Parenteral Therapies, Reduction of Risk Potential, and Physiological Adaptation

CARE ACCORDING TO QUALITY AND SAFETY STANDARDS

Patient-Centered Care

Teamwork and Collaboration

Evidence-Based Practice

Quality Improvement

Safety

Informatics

Buddy Review: _____   Faculty Review: _____

Grade Tracker

Related Exemplars	Related Concepts

Classroom Critical Thinking	Reading / Resources Critical Thinking
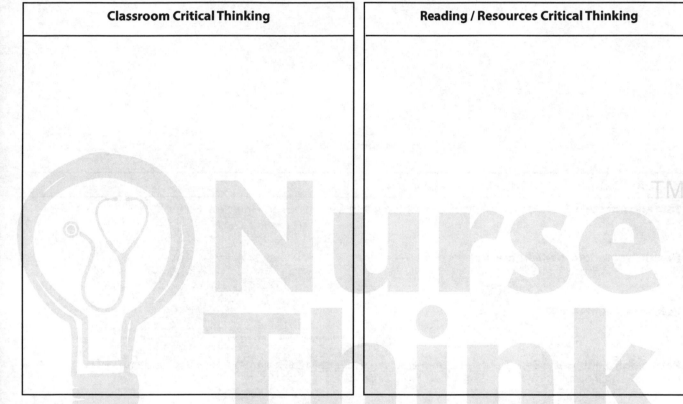	

Priority Assessments	Priority Labs & Diagnostics	Priority Nursing Interventions
1	1	1
2	2	2
3	3	3

Priority Medications	Priority Potential & Actual Complications	Priority Collaborative Goals
1	1	1
2	2	2
3	3	3

NurseThink Quick

CARE ACCORDING TO THE NCLEX® TEST PLAN

Safe and Effective Care: Management of Care, Coordinated Care, Safety and Infection Control

Health Promotion and Maintenance

Psychosocial Integrity

Physiological Integrity: Basic Care and Comfort, Pharmacological and Parenteral Therapies, Reduction of Risk Potential, and Physiological Adaptation

CARE ACCORDING TO QUALITY AND SAFETY STANDARDS

Patient-Centered Care

Teamwork and Collaboration

Evidence-Based Practice

Quality Improvement

Safety

Informatics

Buddy Review: _____   Faculty Review: _____

Grade Tracker

Related Exemplars	**Related Concepts**

Classroom Critical Thinking	**Reading / Resources Critical Thinking**

Priority Assessments

1
2
3

Priority Labs & Diagnostics

1
2
3

Priority Nursing Interventions

1
2
3

Priority Medications

1

2

3

Priority Potential & Actual Complications

1

2

3

Priority Collaborative Goals

1

2

3

NurseThink Quick

UTI- Causing Microorganisms		
Keeps		
Klebsiella		
Enterococcus /Enterobacter		
E-coli		
Pseudomonas/Proteus mirabilis		
Staphylococcus/Serratia		

CARE ACCORDING TO THE NCLEX® TEST PLAN

Safe and Effective Care: Management of Care, Coordinated Care, Safety and Infection Control

Health Promotion and Maintenance

Psychosocial Integrity

Physiological Integrity: Basic Care and Comfort, Pharmacological and Parenteral Therapies, Reduction of Risk Potential, and Physiological Adaptation

CARE ACCORDING TO QUALITY AND SAFETY STANDARDS

Patient-Centered Care

Teamwork and Collaboration

Evidence-Based Practice

Quality Improvement

Safety

Informatics

Buddy Review: _____   Faculty Review: _____

Grade Tracker

Related Exemplars

Related Concepts

Classroom Critical Thinking

Reading / Resources Critical Thinking

Priority Assessments

1
2
3

Priority Labs & Diagnostics

1
2
3

Priority Nursing Interventions

1
2
3

Priority Medications

1

2

3

Priority Potential & Actual Complications

1

2

3

Priority Collaborative Goals

1

2

3

NurseThink Quick

CARE ACCORDING TO THE NCLEX® TEST PLAN

Safe and Effective Care: Management of Care, Coordinated Care, Safety and Infection Control

Health Promotion and Maintenance

Psychosocial Integrity

Physiological Integrity: Basic Care and Comfort, Pharmacological and Parenteral Therapies, Reduction of Risk Potential, and Physiological Adaptation

CARE ACCORDING TO QUALITY AND SAFETY STANDARDS

Patient-Centered Care

Teamwork and Collaboration

Evidence-Based Practice

Quality Improvement

Safety

Informatics

Buddy Review: _____   Faculty Review: _____

Grade Tracker

Related Exemplars

Related Concepts

Classroom Critical Thinking

Reading / Resources Critical Thinking

Priority Assessments

1

2

3

Priority Labs & Diagnostics

1

2

3

Priority Nursing Interventions

1

2

3

Priority Medications

1

2

3

Priority Potential & Actual Complications

1

2

3

Priority Collaborative Goals

1

2

3

NurseThink Quick

CARE ACCORDING TO THE NCLEX® TEST PLAN

Safe and Effective Care: Management of Care, Coordinated Care, Safety and Infection Control

Health Promotion and Maintenance

Psychosocial Integrity

Physiological Integrity: Basic Care and Comfort, Pharmacological and Parenteral Therapies, Reduction of Risk Potential, and Physiological Adaptation

CARE ACCORDING TO QUALITY AND SAFETY STANDARDS

Patient-Centered Care

Teamwork and Collaboration

Evidence-Based Practice

Quality Improvement

Safety

Informatics

Buddy Review: _____   Faculty Review: _____

Grade Tracker

Related Exemplars

Related Concepts

Classroom Critical Thinking

Reading / Resources Critical Thinking

Priority Assessments

1

2

3

Priority Labs & Diagnostics

1

2

3

Priority Nursing Interventions

1

2

3

Priority Medications

1

2

3

Priority Potential & Actual Complications

1

2

3

Priority Collaborative Goals

1

2

3

NurseThink Quick

CARE ACCORDING TO THE NCLEX® TEST PLAN

Safe and Effective Care: Management of Care, Coordinated Care, Safety and Infection Control

Health Promotion and Maintenance

Psychosocial Integrity

Physiological Integrity: Basic Care and Comfort, Pharmacological and Parenteral Therapies, Reduction of Risk Potential, and Physiological Adaptation

CARE ACCORDING TO QUALITY AND SAFETY STANDARDS

Patient-Centered Care

Teamwork and Collaboration

Evidence-Based Practice

Quality Improvement

Safety

Informatics

Buddy Review: _____   Faculty Review: _____

Grade Tracker

Related Exemplars	Related Concepts

Classroom Critical Thinking	Reading / Resources Critical Thinking

Priority Assessments	Priority Labs & Diagnostics	Priority Nursing Interventions
1	1	1
2	2	2
3	3	3

Priority Medications	Priority Potential & Actual Complications	Priority Collaborative Goals
1	1	1
2	2	2
3	3	3

NurseThink Quick

Pneumonia: Risk Factors		
Inspiration **I**mmunosuppression **N**eoplasia **S**ecretion retention **P**ulmonary edema **I**mpaired alveolar macrophages **R**espiratory infection, prior **A**ntibiotics & cytotoxics **T**racheal instrumentation **I**V drug abuse **O**ther (general debility, immobility) **N**eurologic impairment of cough reflex		

CARE ACCORDING TO THE NCLEX® TEST PLAN

Safe and Effective Care: Management of Care, Coordinated Care, Safety and Infection Control

Health Promotion and Maintenance

Psychosocial Integrity

Physiological Integrity: Basic Care and Comfort, Pharmacological and Parenteral Therapies, Reduction of Risk Potential, and Physiological Adaptation

CARE ACCORDING TO QUALITY AND SAFETY STANDARDS

Patient-Centered Care

Teamwork and Collaboration

Evidence-Based Practice

Quality Improvement

Safety

Informatics

Buddy Review: _____   Faculty Review: _____

Grade Tracker

Related Exemplars

Related Concepts

Classroom Critical Thinking

Reading / Resources Critical Thinking

Priority Assessments

1
2
3

Priority Labs & Diagnostics

1
2
3

Priority Nursing Interventions

1
2
3

Priority Medications

1
2
3

Priority Potential & Actual Complications

1
2
3

Priority Collaborative Goals

1
2
3

NurseThink Quick

Anti-TB Drugs and Side Effects

Ripes

Rifampicin – red-orange urine
Isoniazid – peripheral neuritis
Pyrazinamide – increased uric acid
Ethambutol – eye problems
Streptomycin – ototoxic

CARE ACCORDING TO THE NCLEX® TEST PLAN

Safe and Effective Care: Management of Care, Coordinated Care, Safety and Infection Control

Health Promotion and Maintenance

Psychosocial Integrity

Physiological Integrity: Basic Care and Comfort, Pharmacological and Parenteral Therapies, Reduction of Risk Potential, and Physiological Adaptation

CARE ACCORDING TO QUALITY AND SAFETY STANDARDS

Patient-Centered Care

Teamwork and Collaboration

Evidence-Based Practice

Quality Improvement

Safety

Informatics

Buddy Review: _____   Faculty Review: _____

Grade Tracker

Related Exemplars

Related Concepts

Classroom Critical Thinking

Reading / Resources Critical Thinking

Priority Assessments

1
2
3

Priority Labs & Diagnostics

1
2
3

Priority Nursing Interventions

1
2
3

Priority Medications

1
2
3

Priority Potential & Actual Complications

1
2
3

Priority Collaborative Goals

1
2
3

NurseThink Quick

CARE ACCORDING TO THE NCLEX® TEST PLAN

Safe and Effective Care: Management of Care, Coordinated Care, Safety and Infection Control

Health Promotion and Maintenance

Psychosocial Integrity

Physiological Integrity: Basic Care and Comfort, Pharmacological and Parenteral Therapies, Reduction of Risk Potential, and Physiological Adaptation

CARE ACCORDING TO QUALITY AND SAFETY STANDARDS

Patient-Centered Care

Teamwork and Collaboration

Evidence-Based Practice

Quality Improvement

Safety

Informatics

Buddy Review: _____   Faculty Review: _____

Grade Tracker

Related Exemplars	Related Concepts

Classroom Critical Thinking	Reading / Resources Critical Thinking

Priority Assessments	Priority Labs & Diagnostics	Priority Nursing Interventions
1	1	1
2	2	2
3	3	3

Priority Medications	Priority Potential & Actual Complications	Priority Collaborative Goals
1	1	1
2	2	2
3	3	3

NurseThink Quick

CARE ACCORDING TO THE NCLEX® TEST PLAN

Safe and Effective Care: Management of Care, Coordinated Care, Safety and Infection Control

Health Promotion and Maintenance

Psychosocial Integrity

Physiological Integrity: Basic Care and Comfort, Pharmacological and Parenteral Therapies, Reduction of Risk Potential, and Physiological Adaptation

CARE ACCORDING TO QUALITY AND SAFETY STANDARDS

Patient-Centered Care

Teamwork and Collaboration

Evidence-Based Practice

Quality Improvement

Safety

Informatics

Buddy Review: _____   Faculty Review: _____

Grade Tracker

Related Exemplars	**Related Concepts**

Classroom Critical Thinking	**Reading / Resources Critical Thinking**

Priority Assessments

1

2

3

Priority Labs & Diagnostics

1

2

3

Priority Nursing Interventions

1

2

3

Priority Medications

1

2

3

Priority Potential & Actual Complications

1

2

3

Priority Collaborative Goals

1

2

3

NurseThink Quick

Anti-Gout Medications	Gout: Precipitating Factors	Gout: Major Features
Cap Die	*Dark*	*Gout*
Colchicine - **D**eposition of uric acid	**D**iuretics	**G**reat toe
Allopurinol - **I**nhibits uric acid	**A**lcohol	**O**ne joint
Probenecid - **E**xcretion of uric acid	**R**enal disease	**U**ric acid increased
	Kicked (trauma)	**T**ophi

CARE ACCORDING TO THE NCLEX® TEST PLAN

Safe and Effective Care: Management of Care, Coordinated Care, Safety and Infection Control

Health Promotion and Maintenance

Psychosocial Integrity

Physiological Integrity: Basic Care and Comfort, Pharmacological and Parenteral Therapies, Reduction of Risk Potential, and Physiological Adaptation

CARE ACCORDING TO QUALITY AND SAFETY STANDARDS

Patient-Centered Care

Teamwork and Collaboration

Evidence-Based Practice

Quality Improvement

Safety

Informatics

Buddy Review: _____   Faculty Review: _____

Grade Tracker

Related Exemplars

Related Concepts

Classroom Critical Thinking

Reading / Resources Critical Thinking

Priority Assessments

1
2
3

Priority Labs & Diagnostics

1
2
3

Priority Nursing Interventions

1
2
3

Priority Medications

1
2
3

Priority Potential & Actual Complications

1
2
3

Priority Collaborative Goals

1
2
3

NurseThink Quick

CARE ACCORDING TO THE NCLEX® TEST PLAN

Safe and Effective Care: Management of Care, Coordinated Care, Safety and Infection Control

Health Promotion and Maintenance

Psychosocial Integrity

Physiological Integrity: Basic Care and Comfort, Pharmacological and Parenteral Therapies, Reduction of Risk Potential, and Physiological Adaptation

CARE ACCORDING TO QUALITY AND SAFETY STANDARDS

Patient-Centered Care

Teamwork and Collaboration

Evidence-Based Practice

Quality Improvement

Safety

Informatics

Buddy Review: _____   Faculty Review: _____

Grade Tracker

 **Notes**

Iron Deficiency Anemia

Related Exemplars

Related Concepts

Classroom Critical Thinking

Reading / Resources Critical Thinking

Priority Assessments

1
2
3

Priority Labs & Diagnostics

1
2
3

Priority Nursing Interventions

1
2
3

Priority Medications

1
2
3

Priority Potential & Actual Complications

1
2
3

Priority Collaborative Goals

1
2
3

NurseThink Quick

CARE ACCORDING TO THE NCLEX® TEST PLAN

Safe and Effective Care: Management of Care, Coordinated Care, Safety and Infection Control

Health Promotion and Maintenance

Psychosocial Integrity

Physiological Integrity: Basic Care and Comfort, Pharmacological and Parenteral Therapies, Reduction of Risk Potential, and Physiological Adaptation

CARE ACCORDING TO QUALITY AND SAFETY STANDARDS

Patient-Centered Care

Teamwork and Collaboration

Evidence-Based Practice

Quality Improvement

Safety

Informatics

Buddy Review: _____   Faculty Review: _____

Grade Tracker

 **Notes**

Related Exemplars

Related Concepts

Classroom Critical Thinking

Reading / Resources Critical Thinking

Priority Assessments

1
2
3

Priority Labs & Diagnostics

1
2
3

Priority Nursing Interventions

1
2
3

Priority Medications

1
2
3

Priority Potential & Actual Complications

1
2
3

Priority Collaborative Goals

1
2
3

NurseThink Quick

Polycythemia Rubra Vera: Symptoms
PRV
Plethora/Pruritus
Ringing in ears
Visual blurriness

CARE ACCORDING TO THE NCLEX® TEST PLAN

Safe and Effective Care: Management of Care, Coordinated Care, Safety and Infection Control

Health Promotion and Maintenance

Psychosocial Integrity

Physiological Integrity: Basic Care and Comfort, Pharmacological and Parenteral Therapies, Reduction of Risk Potential, and Physiological Adaptation

CARE ACCORDING TO QUALITY AND SAFETY STANDARDS

Patient-Centered Care

Teamwork and Collaboration

Evidence-Based Practice

Quality Improvement

Safety

Informatics

Buddy Review: _____   Faculty Review: _____

Grade Tracker

Related Exemplars

Related Concepts

Classroom Critical Thinking

Reading / Resources Critical Thinking

Priority Assessments

1
2
3

Priority Labs & Diagnostics

1
2
3

Priority Nursing Interventions

1
2
3

Priority Medications

1

2

3

Priority Potential & Actual Complications

1

2

3

Priority Collaborative Goals

1

2

3

NurseThink Quick

CARE ACCORDING TO THE NCLEX® TEST PLAN

Safe and Effective Care: Management of Care, Coordinated Care, Safety and Infection Control

Health Promotion and Maintenance

Psychosocial Integrity

Physiological Integrity: Basic Care and Comfort, Pharmacological and Parenteral Therapies, Reduction of Risk Potential, and Physiological Adaptation

CARE ACCORDING TO QUALITY AND SAFETY STANDARDS

Patient-Centered Care

Teamwork and Collaboration

Evidence-Based Practice

Quality Improvement

Safety

Informatics

Buddy Review: _____   Faculty Review: _____

Grade Tracker

Related Exemplars	Related Concepts

Classroom Critical Thinking	Reading / Resources Critical Thinking

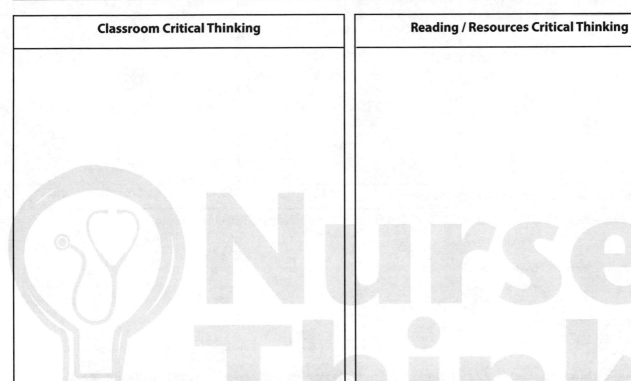

Priority Assessments

1
2
3

Priority Labs & Diagnostics

1
2
3

Priority Nursing Interventions

1
2
3

Priority Medications

1

2

3

Priority Potential & Actual Complications

1

2

3

Priority Collaborative Goals

1

2

3

NurseThink Quick

Bleeding Disorders: Signs and Symptoms	Thrombotic Thrombocytopenic Purpura: Signs	TTP: Clinical Features

Bleeding Disorders: Signs and Symptoms

Beep
Bleeding gums
Ecchymosis (bruises)
Epistaxis (nosebleed)
Petechiae (tiny purplish spots)

Thrombotic Thrombocytopenic Purpura: Signs

Fat RN
Fever
Anemia
Thrombocytopenia
Renal problems
Neurologic dysfunction

TTP: Clinical Features

Partner
Platelet count low
Anemia
Renal failure
Temperature rise
Neurological deficits
ER admission

CARE ACCORDING TO THE NCLEX® TEST PLAN

Safe and Effective Care: Management of Care, Coordinated Care, Safety and Infection Control

Health Promotion and Maintenance

Psychosocial Integrity

Physiological Integrity: Basic Care and Comfort, Pharmacological and Parenteral Therapies, Reduction of Risk Potential, and Physiological Adaptation

CARE ACCORDING TO QUALITY AND SAFETY STANDARDS

Patient-Centered Care

Teamwork and Collaboration

Evidence-Based Practice

Quality Improvement

Safety

Informatics

Buddy Review: _____   Faculty Review: _____

Grade Tracker

Related Exemplars

Related Concepts

Classroom Critical Thinking

Reading / Resources Critical Thinking

Priority Assessments

1
2
3

Priority Labs & Diagnostics

1
2
3

Priority Nursing Interventions

1
2
3

Priority Medications

1
2
3

Priority Potential & Actual Complications

1
2
3

Priority Collaborative Goals

1
2
3

NurseThink Quick

CARE ACCORDING TO THE NCLEX® TEST PLAN

Safe and Effective Care: Management of Care, Coordinated Care, Safety and Infection Control

Health Promotion and Maintenance

Psychosocial Integrity

Physiological Integrity: Basic Care and Comfort, Pharmacological and Parenteral Therapies, Reduction of Risk Potential, and Physiological Adaptation

CARE ACCORDING TO QUALITY AND SAFETY STANDARDS

Patient-Centered Care

Teamwork and Collaboration

Evidence-Based Practice

Quality Improvement

Safety

Informatics

Buddy Review: _____   Faculty Review: _____

Grade Tracker

Related Exemplars

Related Concepts

Classroom Critical Thinking

Reading / Resources Critical Thinking

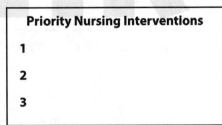

Priority Assessments

1
2
3

Priority Labs & Diagnostics

1
2
3

Priority Nursing Interventions

1
2
3

Priority Medications

1

2

3

Priority Potential & Actual Complications

1

2

3

Priority Collaborative Goals

1

2

3

 **Notes**

NurseThink Quick

Carcinomas that Metastasize to Bone
Particular Tumors Love Killing Bone
Prostate
Thyroid
Lung
Kidney
Breast

CARE ACCORDING TO THE NCLEX® TEST PLAN

Safe and Effective Care: Management of Care, Coordinated Care, Safety and Infection Control

Health Promotion and Maintenance

Psychosocial Integrity

Physiological Integrity: Basic Care and Comfort, Pharmacological and Parenteral Therapies, Reduction of Risk Potential, and Physiological Adaptation

CARE ACCORDING TO QUALITY AND SAFETY STANDARDS

Patient-Centered Care

Teamwork and Collaboration

Evidence-Based Practice

Quality Improvement

Safety

Informatics

Buddy Review: _____   Faculty Review: _____

Grade Tracker

Related Exemplars	**Related Concepts**

Classroom Critical Thinking	**Reading / Resources Critical Thinking**
	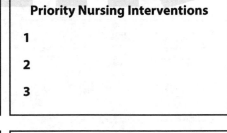

Priority Assessments

1
2
3

Priority Labs & Diagnostics

1
2
3

Priority Nursing Interventions

1
2
3

Priority Medications

1

2

3

Priority Potential & Actual Complications

1

2

3

Priority Collaborative Goals

1

2

3

NurseThink Quick

CARE ACCORDING TO THE NCLEX® TEST PLAN

Safe and Effective Care: Management of Care, Coordinated Care, Safety and Infection Control

Health Promotion and Maintenance

Psychosocial Integrity

Physiological Integrity: Basic Care and Comfort, Pharmacological and Parenteral Therapies, Reduction of Risk Potential, and Physiological Adaptation

CARE ACCORDING TO QUALITY AND SAFETY STANDARDS

Patient-Centered Care

Teamwork and Collaboration

Evidence-Based Practice

Quality Improvement

Safety

Informatics

Buddy Review: _____   Faculty Review: _____

Grade Tracker

Related Exemplars

Related Concepts

Classroom Critical Thinking

Reading / Resources Critical Thinking

Priority Assessments

1
2
3

Priority Labs & Diagnostics

1
2
3

Priority Nursing Interventions

1
2
3

Priority Medications

1

2

3

Priority Potential & Actual Complications

1

2

3

Priority Collaborative Goals

1

2

3

NurseThink Quick

Breast Self-Examination Song
Tune of 3 little Indians
♫ ♪ ♪ ♫ 1 little 2, little 3 little fingers Do BSE 7 days after menses
Press nipple once for discharge, call your doctor
I'm sure you will do it more...♫ ♪ ♪

CARE ACCORDING TO THE NCLEX® TEST PLAN

Safe and Effective Care: Management of Care, Coordinated Care, Safety and Infection Control

Health Promotion and Maintenance

Psychosocial Integrity

Physiological Integrity: Basic Care and Comfort, Pharmacological and Parenteral Therapies, Reduction of Risk Potential, and Physiological Adaptation

CARE ACCORDING TO QUALITY AND SAFETY STANDARDS

Patient-Centered Care

Teamwork and Collaboration

Evidence-Based Practice

Quality Improvement

Safety

Informatics

Buddy Review: _____   Faculty Review: _____

Grade Tracker

Related Exemplars	**Related Concepts**

Classroom Critical Thinking	**Reading / Resources Critical Thinking**

Priority Assessments

1
2
3

Priority Labs & Diagnostics

1
2
3

Priority Nursing Interventions

1
2
3

Priority Medications

1
2
3

Priority Potential & Actual Complications

1
2
3

Priority Collaborative Goals

1
2
3

NurseThink Quick

Colon Carcinoma: Causes	Colon Cancer: Risk Factors	
Craps	***Hula***	
Chronic ulcerative colitis	**H**eredity/Hereditary diseases	
Ratio of animal fat to fiber diet A – Adenomatous polyps	**U**lcerative colitis	
Polyposis (Familial)	**L**ow-fiber, high-fat diet	
Strong family history of colon cancer	**A**denomatous polyps	

CARE ACCORDING TO THE NCLEX® TEST PLAN

Safe and Effective Care: Management of Care, Coordinated Care, Safety and Infection Control

Health Promotion and Maintenance

Psychosocial Integrity

Physiological Integrity: Basic Care and Comfort, Pharmacological and Parenteral Therapies, Reduction of Risk Potential, and Physiological Adaptation

CARE ACCORDING TO QUALITY AND SAFETY STANDARDS

Patient-Centered Care

Teamwork and Collaboration

Evidence-Based Practice

Quality Improvement

Safety

Informatics

Buddy Review: _____   Faculty Review: _____

Grade Tracker

Related Exemplars

Related Concepts

Classroom Critical Thinking

Reading / Resources Critical Thinking

Priority Assessments
1
2
3

Priority Labs & Diagnostics
1
2
3

Priority Nursing Interventions
1
2
3

Priority Medications
1

2

3

Priority Potential & Actual Complications
1

2

3

Priority Collaborative Goals
1

2

3

NurseThink Quick

CARE ACCORDING TO THE NCLEX® TEST PLAN

Safe and Effective Care: Management of Care, Coordinated Care, Safety and Infection Control

Health Promotion and Maintenance

Psychosocial Integrity

Physiological Integrity: Basic Care and Comfort, Pharmacological and Parenteral Therapies, Reduction of Risk Potential, and Physiological Adaptation

CARE ACCORDING TO QUALITY AND SAFETY STANDARDS

Patient-Centered Care

Teamwork and Collaboration

Evidence-Based Practice

Quality Improvement

Safety

Informatics

Buddy Review: _____   Faculty Review: _____

Grade Tracker

Related Exemplars

Related Concepts

Classroom Critical Thinking

Reading / Resources Critical Thinking

Priority Assessments

1
2
3

Priority Labs & Diagnostics

1
2
3

Priority Nursing Interventions

1
2
3

Priority Medications

1
2
3

Priority Potential & Actual Complications

1
2
3

Priority Collaborative Goals

1
2
3

NurseThink Notes

NurseThink Quick

CARE ACCORDING TO THE NCLEX® TEST PLAN

Safe and Effective Care: Management of Care, Coordinated Care, Safety and Infection Control

Health Promotion and Maintenance

Psychosocial Integrity

Physiological Integrity: Basic Care and Comfort, Pharmacological and Parenteral Therapies, Reduction of Risk Potential, and Physiological Adaptation

CARE ACCORDING TO QUALITY AND SAFETY STANDARDS

Patient-Centered Care

Teamwork and Collaboration

Evidence-Based Practice

Quality Improvement

Safety

Informatics

Buddy Review: _____   Faculty Review: _____

Grade Tracker

Related Exemplars

Related Concepts

Classroom Critical Thinking

Reading / Resources Critical Thinking

Priority Assessments
1
2
3

Priority Labs & Diagnostics
1
2
3

Priority Nursing Interventions
1
2
3

Priority Medications
1

2

3

Priority Potential & Actual Complications
1

2

3

Priority Collaborative Goals
1

2

3

NurseThink Quick

CARE ACCORDING TO THE NCLEX® TEST PLAN

Safe and Effective Care: Management of Care, Coordinated Care, Safety and Infection Control

Health Promotion and Maintenance

Psychosocial Integrity

Physiological Integrity: Basic Care and Comfort, Pharmacological and Parenteral Therapies, Reduction of Risk Potential, and Physiological Adaptation

CARE ACCORDING TO QUALITY AND SAFETY STANDARDS

Patient-Centered Care

Teamwork and Collaboration

Evidence-Based Practice

Quality Improvement

Safety

Informatics

Buddy Review: _____   Faculty Review: _____

Grade Tracker

Related Exemplars	Related Concepts

Classroom Critical Thinking	Reading / Resources Critical Thinking

Priority Assessments	Priority Labs & Diagnostics	Priority Nursing Interventions
1	1	1
2	2	2
3	3	3

Priority Medications	Priority Potential & Actual Complications	Priority Collaborative Goals
1	1	1
2	2	2
3	3	3

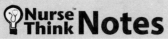
NurseThink Quick

Lymphoma: Staging of B-Cell CLL (RAI)		
Lymphoma: Staging of B-Cell CLL (RAI) *LOATh* I: **L**ymphadenopathy II: **O**rganomegaly (splenomegaly) III: **A**nemia IV: **Th**rombocytopenia		

CARE ACCORDING TO THE NCLEX® TEST PLAN

Safe and Effective Care: Management of Care, Coordinated Care, Safety and Infection Control

Health Promotion and Maintenance

Psychosocial Integrity

Physiological Integrity: Basic Care and Comfort, Pharmacological and Parenteral Therapies, Reduction of Risk Potential, and Physiological Adaptation

CARE ACCORDING TO QUALITY AND SAFETY STANDARDS

Patient-Centered Care

Teamwork and Collaboration

Evidence-Based Practice

Quality Improvement

Safety

Informatics

Buddy Review: _____   Faculty Review: _____

Grade Tracker

Related Exemplars

Related Concepts

Classroom Critical Thinking

Reading / Resources Critical Thinking

Priority Assessments

1

2

3

Priority Labs & Diagnostics

1

2

3

Priority Nursing Interventions

1

2

3

Priority Medications

1

2

3

Priority Potential & Actual Complications

1

2

3

Priority Collaborative Goals

1

2

3

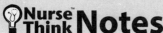
NurseThink Quick

Multiple Myeloma: Symptoms
BAHRAIN UV
Bone Pain
Anemia
Hypercalcemia
Renal failure
Amyloidosis
Infection
Neuropathy
Uricaemia
Viscosity

CARE ACCORDING TO THE NCLEX® TEST PLAN

Safe and Effective Care: Management of Care, Coordinated Care, Safety and Infection Control

Health Promotion and Maintenance

Psychosocial Integrity

Physiological Integrity: Basic Care and Comfort, Pharmacological and Parenteral Therapies, Reduction of Risk Potential, and Physiological Adaptation

CARE ACCORDING TO QUALITY AND SAFETY STANDARDS

Patient-Centered Care

Teamwork and Collaboration

Evidence-Based Practice

Quality Improvement

Safety

Informatics

Buddy Review: _____   Faculty Review: _____

Grade Tracker

Related Exemplars	Related Concepts

Classroom Critical Thinking	Reading / Resources Critical Thinking

Priority Assessments

1
2
3

Priority Labs & Diagnostics

1
2
3

Priority Nursing Interventions

1
2
3

Priority Medications

1
2
3

Priority Potential & Actual Complications

1
2
3

Priority Collaborative Goals

1
2
3

NurseThink Quick

CARE ACCORDING TO THE NCLEX® TEST PLAN

Safe and Effective Care: Management of Care, Coordinated Care, Safety and Infection Control

Health Promotion and Maintenance

Psychosocial Integrity

Physiological Integrity: Basic Care and Comfort, Pharmacological and Parenteral Therapies, Reduction of Risk Potential, and Physiological Adaptation

CARE ACCORDING TO QUALITY AND SAFETY STANDARDS

Patient-Centered Care

Teamwork and Collaboration

Evidence-Based Practice

Quality Improvement

Safety

Informatics

Buddy Review: _____   Faculty Review: _____

Grade Tracker

Related Exemplars	**Related Concepts**

Classroom Critical Thinking	**Reading / Resources Critical Thinking**

Priority Assessments	**Priority Labs & Diagnostics**	**Priority Nursing Interventions**
1	1	1
2	2	2
3	3	3

Priority Medications	**Priority Potential & Actual Complications**	**Priority Collaborative Goals**
1	1	1
2	2	2
3	3	3

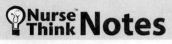

NurseThink Quick

Malignant Mole: Signs and Symptoms	Malignant Melanoma: 3 sites with poor prognosis	
ABCD	**Bans**	
Asymmetry: is the mole irregular in shape?	**B**ack of arm	
Border: is the border irregular, notched, or poorly defined?	**N**eck	
Color: does the color vary	**S**calp	
Diameter: is the diameter more than 6 mm?		

CARE ACCORDING TO THE NCLEX® TEST PLAN

Safe and Effective Care: Management of Care, Coordinated Care, Safety and Infection Control

Health Promotion and Maintenance

Psychosocial Integrity

Physiological Integrity: Basic Care and Comfort, Pharmacological and Parenteral Therapies, Reduction of Risk Potential, and Physiological Adaptation

CARE ACCORDING TO QUALITY AND SAFETY STANDARDS

Patient-Centered Care

Teamwork and Collaboration

Evidence-Based Practice

Quality Improvement

Safety

Informatics

Buddy Review: _____   Faculty Review: _____

Grade Tracker

Nurse Think Notes

Related Exemplars

Related Concepts

Classroom Critical Thinking

Reading / Resources Critical Thinking

Priority Assessments

1

2

3

Priority Labs & Diagnostics

1

2

3

Priority Nursing Interventions

1

2

3

Priority Medications

1

2

3

Priority Potential & Actual Complications

1

2

3

Priority Collaborative Goals

1

2

3

NurseThink Quick

ICP waveforms	Increased ICP: Cushing's Triad	
ABC's	***Hyper-Brady-Brady***	
A is Awful	**Hypertension** (wise pulse pressure)	
B is Bad	**Bradycardia**	
C is Common	**Bradypnea**	

CARE ACCORDING TO THE NCLEX® TEST PLAN

Safe and Effective Care: Management of Care, Coordinated Care, Safety and Infection Control

Health Promotion and Maintenance

Psychosocial Integrity

Physiological Integrity: Basic Care and Comfort, Pharmacological and Parenteral Therapies, Reduction of Risk Potential, and Physiological Adaptation

CARE ACCORDING TO QUALITY AND SAFETY STANDARDS

Patient-Centered Care

Teamwork and Collaboration

Evidence-Based Practice

Quality Improvement

Safety

Informatics

Buddy Review: _____   Faculty Review: _____

Grade Tracker

Related Exemplars

Related Concepts

Classroom Critical Thinking

Reading / Resources Critical Thinking

Priority Assessments

1

2

3

Priority Labs & Diagnostics

1

2

3

Priority Nursing Interventions

1

2

3

Priority Medications

1

2

3

Priority Potential & Actual Complications

1

2

3

Priority Collaborative Goals

1

2

3

NurseThink Quick

CARE ACCORDING TO THE NCLEX® TEST PLAN

Safe and Effective Care: Management of Care, Coordinated Care, Safety and Infection Control

Health Promotion and Maintenance

Psychosocial Integrity

Physiological Integrity: Basic Care and Comfort, Pharmacological and Parenteral Therapies, Reduction of Risk Potential, and Physiological Adaptation

CARE ACCORDING TO QUALITY AND SAFETY STANDARDS

Patient-Centered Care

Teamwork and Collaboration

Evidence-Based Practice

Quality Improvement

Safety

Informatics

Buddy Review: _____   Faculty Review: _____

Grade Tracker

Related Exemplars

Related Concepts

Classroom Critical Thinking

Reading / Resources Critical Thinking

Priority Assessments

1
2
3

Priority Labs & Diagnostics

1
2
3

Priority Nursing Interventions

1
2
3

Priority Medications

1
2
3

Priority Potential & Actual Complications

1
2
3

Priority Collaborative Goals

1
2
3

NurseThink Quick

<table>
<tr><td></td><td></td><td></td></tr>
</table>

CARE ACCORDING TO THE NCLEX® TEST PLAN

Safe and Effective Care: Management of Care, Coordinated Care, Safety and Infection Control

Health Promotion and Maintenance

Psychosocial Integrity

Physiological Integrity: Basic Care and Comfort, Pharmacological and Parenteral Therapies, Reduction of Risk Potential, and Physiological Adaptation

CARE ACCORDING TO QUALITY AND SAFETY STANDARDS

Patient-Centered Care

Teamwork and Collaboration

Evidence-Based Practice

Quality Improvement

Safety

Informatics

Buddy Review: _____   Faculty Review: _____

Grade Tracker

<table>
<tr><td></td><td></td><td></td><td></td><td></td><td></td><td></td><td></td><td></td><td></td><td></td><td></td><td></td><td></td><td></td><td></td><td></td><td></td></tr>
</table>

Related Exemplars

Related Concepts

Classroom Critical Thinking

Reading / Resources Critical Thinking

Priority Assessments

1
2
3

Priority Labs & Diagnostics

1
2
3

Priority Nursing Interventions

1
2
3

Priority Medications

1
2
3

Priority Potential & Actual Complications

1
2
3

Priority Collaborative Goals

1
2
3

NurseThink Quick

CARE ACCORDING TO THE NCLEX® TEST PLAN

Safe and Effective Care: Management of Care, Coordinated Care, Safety and Infection Control

Health Promotion and Maintenance

Psychosocial Integrity

Physiological Integrity: Basic Care and Comfort, Pharmacological and Parenteral Therapies, Reduction of Risk Potential, and Physiological Adaptation

CARE ACCORDING TO QUALITY AND SAFETY STANDARDS

Patient-Centered Care

Teamwork and Collaboration

Evidence-Based Practice

Quality Improvement

Safety

Informatics

Buddy Review: _____   Faculty Review: _____

Grade Tracker

Related Exemplars

Related Concepts

Classroom Critical Thinking

Reading / Resources Critical Thinking

Priority Assessments

1
2
3

Priority Labs & Diagnostics

1
2
3

Priority Nursing Interventions

1
2
3

Priority Medications

1
2
3

Priority Potential & Actual Complications

1
2
3

Priority Collaborative Goals

1
2
3

NurseThink Quick

CARE ACCORDING TO THE NCLEX® TEST PLAN

Safe and Effective Care: Management of Care, Coordinated Care, Safety and Infection Control

Health Promotion and Maintenance

Psychosocial Integrity

Physiological Integrity: Basic Care and Comfort, Pharmacological and Parenteral Therapies, Reduction of Risk Potential, and Physiological Adaptation

CARE ACCORDING TO QUALITY AND SAFETY STANDARDS

Patient-Centered Care

Teamwork and Collaboration

Evidence-Based Practice

Quality Improvement

Safety

Informatics

Buddy Review: _____   Faculty Review: _____

Grade Tracker

Related Exemplars	**Related Concepts**

Classroom Critical Thinking	**Reading / Resources Critical Thinking**

Priority Assessments

1
2
3

Priority Labs & Diagnostics

1
2
3

Priority Nursing Interventions

1
2
3

Priority Medications

1

2

3

Priority Potential & Actual Complications

1

2

3

Priority Collaborative Goals

1

2

3

NurseThink Quick

Hepatitis: Transmission Routes		
Vowels are Bowels Hepatitis A and E transmitted by fecal- oral route		

CARE ACCORDING TO THE NCLEX® TEST PLAN

Safe and Effective Care: Management of Care, Coordinated Care, Safety and Infection Control

Health Promotion and Maintenance

Psychosocial Integrity

Physiological Integrity: Basic Care and Comfort, Pharmacological and Parenteral Therapies, Reduction of Risk Potential, and Physiological Adaptation

CARE ACCORDING TO QUALITY AND SAFETY STANDARDS

Patient-Centered Care

Teamwork and Collaboration

Evidence-Based Practice

Quality Improvement

Safety

Informatics

Buddy Review: _____   Faculty Review: _____

Grade Tracker

Related Exemplars	Related Concepts

Classroom Critical Thinking	Reading / Resources Critical Thinking

Priority Assessments

1
2
3

Priority Labs & Diagnostics

1
2
3

Priority Nursing Interventions

1
2
3

Priority Medications

1

2

3

Priority Potential & Actual Complications

1

2

3

Priority Collaborative Goals

1

2

3

NurseThink Quick

Hepatotoxic Drugs	Elevated ALT or AST Values	Liver Failure
8 A's and SGPT/SGOT	**ABCDEFGHIM**	**Claps**
Antituberculosis	**A**utoimmune hepatitis	**C**lubbing
Anticonvulsant	**H**epatitis **B**	**L**eukonychia
Sodium luminal	**H**epatitis **C**	**A**sterixis
Gabapentin	**D**rugs or toxins	**P**almar Erythema
Phenytoin	**E**thanol	**S**cratch marks
Tegretol	**F**atty liver	
Anticancer	**G**rowths of tumors	
Aspirin	**H**emodynamic disorder	
Alcohol	**I**ron or copper deficiency	
Antifamily (contraceptive pills)	**M**uscle Injury	
Acetaminophen		
Aflatoxins		

CARE ACCORDING TO THE NCLEX® TEST PLAN

Safe and Effective Care: Management of Care, Coordinated Care, Safety and Infection Control

Health Promotion and Maintenance

Psychosocial Integrity

Physiological Integrity: Basic Care and Comfort, Pharmacological and Parenteral Therapies, Reduction of Risk Potential, and Physiological Adaptation

CARE ACCORDING TO QUALITY AND SAFETY STANDARDS

Patient-Centered Care

Teamwork and Collaboration

Evidence-Based Practice

Quality Improvement

Safety

Informatics

Buddy Review: _____   Faculty Review: _____

Grade Tracker

Related Exemplars

Related Concepts

Classroom Critical Thinking

Reading / Resources Critical Thinking

Priority Assessments

1

2

3

Priority Labs & Diagnostics

1

2

3

Priority Nursing Interventions

1

2

3

Priority Medications

1

2

3

Priority Potential & Actual Complications

1

2

3

Priority Collaborative Goals

1

2

3

NurseThink Quick

Addison's Causes	President Kennedy had Addison's Disease: He always had a great tan. A President would need cortisol to respond to stress and hypoglycemia.	
Antam **A**utoimmune **N**eoplastic **T**B **A**myloid **M**eningococcal		

CARE ACCORDING TO THE NCLEX® TEST PLAN

Safe and Effective Care: Management of Care, Coordinated Care, Safety and Infection Control

Health Promotion and Maintenance

Psychosocial Integrity

Physiological Integrity: Basic Care and Comfort, Pharmacological and Parenteral Therapies, Reduction of Risk Potential, and Physiological Adaptation

CARE ACCORDING TO QUALITY AND SAFETY STANDARDS

Patient-Centered Care

Teamwork and Collaboration

Evidence-Based Practice

Quality Improvement

Safety

Informatics

Buddy Review: _____   Faculty Review: _____

Grade Tracker

Related Exemplars	Related Concepts

Classroom Critical Thinking	Reading / Resources Critical Thinking

Priority Assessments
1
2
3

Priority Labs & Diagnostics
1
2
3

Priority Nursing Interventions
1
2
3

Priority Medications
1
2
3

Priority Potential & Actual Complications
1
2
3

Priority Collaborative Goals
1
2
3

NurseThink Quick

Cushing Symptoms	Cushing Syndrome	
3 S's	***Cushing***	
Sugar (hyperglycemia)	**C**entral obesity	
Salt (hypernatremia)	**U**rinary free cortisol and glucose increase	
Sex (excess androgens)	**S**triate/Suppressed immunity	
	Hypercortisolism/Hypertension/ Hyper-glycemia/ Hirsuism	
	Iatrogenic (Increased administration of corticosteroids)	
	Noniatrogenic (Neoplasms)	
	Glucose intolerance/ Growth retardation	

CARE ACCORDING TO THE NCLEX® TEST PLAN

Safe and Effective Care: Management of Care, Coordinated Care, Safety and Infection Control

Health Promotion and Maintenance

Psychosocial Integrity

Physiological Integrity: Basic Care and Comfort, Pharmacological and Parenteral Therapies, Reduction of Risk Potential, and Physiological Adaptation

CARE ACCORDING TO QUALITY AND SAFETY STANDARDS

Patient-Centered Care

Teamwork and Collaboration

Evidence-Based Practice

Quality Improvement

Safety

Informatics

Buddy Review: _____   Faculty Review: _____

Grade Tracker

Related Exemplars

Related Concepts

Classroom Critical Thinking

Reading / Resources Critical Thinking

Priority Assessments

1
2
3

Priority Labs & Diagnostics

1
2
3

Priority Nursing Interventions

1
2
3

Priority Medications

1
2
3

Priority Potential & Actual Complications

1
2
3

Priority Collaborative Goals

1
2
3

NurseThink Quick

Crohn's Disease Symptoms
Christmas
Cobblestones
High temperature
Reduced lumen
Intestinal fistulae
Skip lesions
Transmural
Malabsorption
Abdominal pain
Submucosal fibrosis

CARE ACCORDING TO THE NCLEX® TEST PLAN

Safe and Effective Care: Management of Care, Coordinated Care, Safety and Infection Control

Health Promotion and Maintenance

Psychosocial Integrity

Physiological Integrity: Basic Care and Comfort, Pharmacological and Parenteral Therapies, Reduction of Risk Potential, and Physiological Adaptation

CARE ACCORDING TO QUALITY AND SAFETY STANDARDS

Patient-Centered Care

Teamwork and Collaboration

Evidence-Based Practice

Quality Improvement

Safety

Informatics

Buddy Review: _____   Faculty Review: _____

Grade Tracker

Related Exemplars	Related Concepts

Classroom Critical Thinking	Reading / Resources Critical Thinking

Priority Assessments

1
2
3

Priority Labs & Diagnostics

1
2
3

Priority Nursing Interventions

1
2
3

Priority Medications

1
2
3

Priority Potential & Actual Complications

1
2
3

Priority Collaborative Goals

1
2
3

NurseThink Quick

CARE ACCORDING TO THE NCLEX® TEST PLAN

Safe and Effective Care: Management of Care, Coordinated Care, Safety and Infection Control

Health Promotion and Maintenance

Psychosocial Integrity

Physiological Integrity: Basic Care and Comfort, Pharmacological and Parenteral Therapies, Reduction of Risk Potential, and Physiological Adaptation

CARE ACCORDING TO QUALITY AND SAFETY STANDARDS

Patient-Centered Care

Teamwork and Collaboration

Evidence-Based Practice

Quality Improvement

Safety

Informatics

Buddy Review: _____   Faculty Review: _____

Grade Tracker

Related Exemplars

Related Concepts

Classroom Critical Thinking

Reading / Resources Critical Thinking

Priority Assessments

1

2

3

Priority Labs & Diagnostics

1

2

3

Priority Nursing Interventions

1

2

3

Priority Medications

1

2

3

Priority Potential & Actual Complications

1

2

3

Priority Collaborative Goals

1

2

3

NurseThink Notes

NurseThink Quick

GI Obstruction: Symptoms	Small Bowel Obstruction: Causes	
PV D & C **P**ain **V**omiting **D**istension **C**onstipation	*Shavit* **S**tone **H**ernia **A**dhesions **V**olvulus **I**ntussusception **T**umor	

CARE ACCORDING TO THE NCLEX® TEST PLAN

Safe and Effective Care: Management of Care, Coordinated Care, Safety and Infection Control

Health Promotion and Maintenance

Psychosocial Integrity

Physiological Integrity: Basic Care and Comfort, Pharmacological and Parenteral Therapies, Reduction of Risk Potential, and Physiological Adaptation

CARE ACCORDING TO QUALITY AND SAFETY STANDARDS

Patient-Centered Care

Teamwork and Collaboration

Evidence-Based Practice

Quality Improvement

Safety

Informatics

Buddy Review: _____   Faculty Review: _____

Grade Tracker

Related Exemplars	Related Concepts

Classroom Critical Thinking	Reading / Resources Critical Thinking

Priority Assessments

1
2
3

Priority Labs & Diagnostics

1
2
3

Priority Nursing Interventions

1
2
3

Priority Medications

1

2

3

Priority Potential & Actual Complications

1

2

3

Priority Collaborative Goals

1

2

3

NurseThink Quick

IBD: Surgery Indications
I Chop
Infection
Carcinoma
Hemorrhage
Obstruction
Perforation

CARE ACCORDING TO THE NCLEX® TEST PLAN

Safe and Effective Care: Management of Care, Coordinated Care, Safety and Infection Control

Health Promotion and Maintenance

Psychosocial Integrity

Physiological Integrity: Basic Care and Comfort, Pharmacological and Parenteral Therapies, Reduction of Risk Potential, and Physiological Adaptation

CARE ACCORDING TO QUALITY AND SAFETY STANDARDS

Patient-Centered Care

Teamwork and Collaboration

Evidence-Based Practice

Quality Improvement

Safety

Informatics

Buddy Review: _____   Faculty Review: _____

Grade Tracker

Related Exemplars

Related Concepts

Classroom Critical Thinking

Reading / Resources Critical Thinking

Priority Assessments

1

2

3

Priority Labs & Diagnostics

1

2

3

Priority Nursing Interventions

1

2

3

Priority Medications

1

2

3

Priority Potential & Actual Complications

1

2

3

Priority Collaborative Goals

1

2

3

NurseThink Quick

CARE ACCORDING TO THE NCLEX® TEST PLAN

Safe and Effective Care: Management of Care, Coordinated Care, Safety and Infection Control

Health Promotion and Maintenance

Psychosocial Integrity

Physiological Integrity: Basic Care and Comfort, Pharmacological and Parenteral Therapies, Reduction of Risk Potential, and Physiological Adaptation

CARE ACCORDING TO QUALITY AND SAFETY STANDARDS

Patient-Centered Care

Teamwork and Collaboration

Evidence-Based Practice

Quality Improvement

Safety

Informatics

Buddy Review: _____   Faculty Review: _____

Grade Tracker

Related Exemplars	Related Concepts

Classroom Critical Thinking	Reading / Resources Critical Thinking

Priority Assessments	Priority Labs & Diagnostics	Priority Nursing Interventions
1	1	1
2	2	2
3	3	3

Priority Medications	Priority Potential & Actual Complications	Priority Collaborative Goals
1	1	1
2	2	2
3	3	3

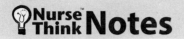

NurseThink Quick

Ulcerative Colitis: Definition of a severe attack **A State** **A**nemia less than 10 g/dL **S**tool frequency greater than 6 stills/day with blood **T**emperature greater than 37.5 **A**lbumin less than 30g/L **T**achycardia greater than 90bpm **E**SR greater than 30 mm/hr	**Ulcerative Colitis: Complications** *Past Colitis* **P**yoderma gangrenosum **A**nkylosing spondylitis **S**clerosing pericholangities **T**oxic megacolon **C**olon carcinoma	

CARE ACCORDING TO THE NCLEX® TEST PLAN

Safe and Effective Care: Management of Care, Coordinated Care, Safety and Infection Control

Health Promotion and Maintenance

Psychosocial Integrity

Physiological Integrity: Basic Care and Comfort, Pharmacological and Parenteral Therapies, Reduction of Risk Potential, and Physiological Adaptation

CARE ACCORDING TO QUALITY AND SAFETY STANDARDS

Patient-Centered Care

Teamwork and Collaboration

Evidence-Based Practice

Quality Improvement

Safety

Informatics

Buddy Review: _____   Faculty Review: _____

Grade Tracker

Related Exemplars

Related Concepts

Classroom Critical Thinking

Reading / Resources Critical Thinking

Priority Assessments

1

2

3

Priority Labs & Diagnostics

1

2

3

Priority Nursing Interventions

1

2

3

Priority Medications

1

2

3

Priority Potential & Actual Complications

1

2

3

Priority Collaborative Goals

1

2

3

🔦 NurseThink Notes

NurseThink Quick

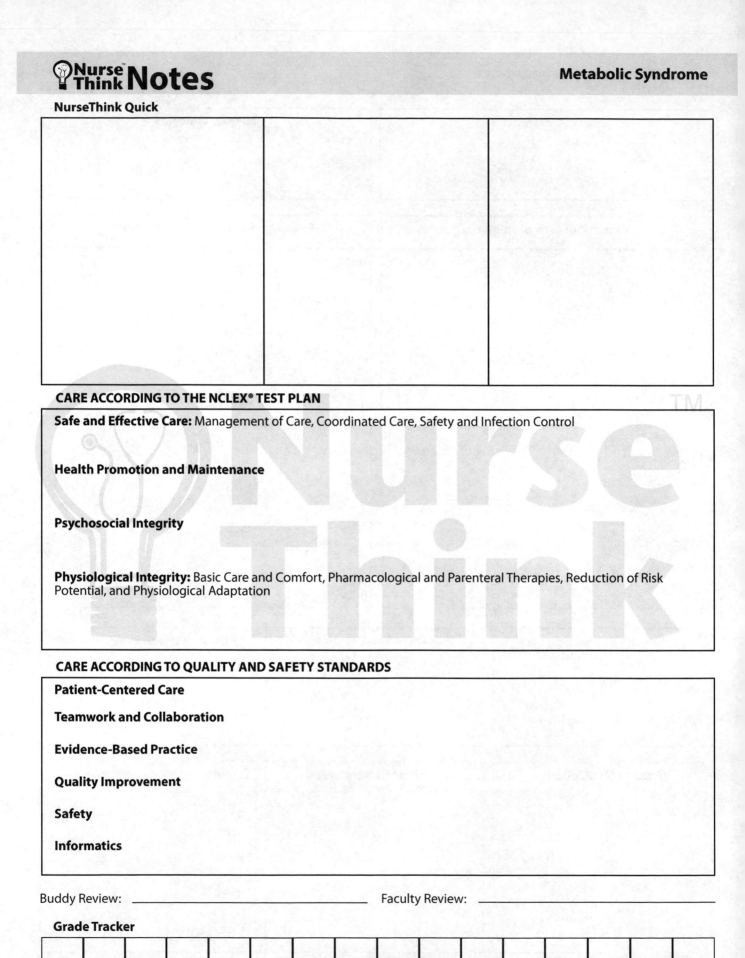

CARE ACCORDING TO THE NCLEX® TEST PLAN

Safe and Effective Care: Management of Care, Coordinated Care, Safety and Infection Control

Health Promotion and Maintenance

Psychosocial Integrity

Physiological Integrity: Basic Care and Comfort, Pharmacological and Parenteral Therapies, Reduction of Risk Potential, and Physiological Adaptation

CARE ACCORDING TO QUALITY AND SAFETY STANDARDS

Patient-Centered Care

Teamwork and Collaboration

Evidence-Based Practice

Quality Improvement

Safety

Informatics

Buddy Review: _____   Faculty Review: _____

Grade Tracker

Related Exemplars

Related Concepts

Classroom Critical Thinking

Reading / Resources Critical Thinking

Priority Assessments

1
2
3

Priority Labs & Diagnostics

1
2
3

Priority Nursing Interventions

1
2
3

Priority Medications

1
2
3

Priority Potential & Actual Complications

1
2
3

Priority Collaborative Goals

1
2
3

NurseThink Quick

Hyperglycemia
(Skin) Hot and Dry: sugar's high
(Skin) Cold and Clammy: need some candy

Diabetes: Signs and Symptoms
3 P's
Polydipsia
Polyphagia
Polyuria

Diabetes Complications
Knives
Kidney
Neuropathy
Infection
Vascular
Eyes
Skin lesions

Diabetic Ketoacidosis: Treatment
Fire
Fluids
Insulin
Replace
Electrolytes

CARE ACCORDING TO THE NCLEX® TEST PLAN

Safe and Effective Care: Management of Care, Coordinated Care, Safety and Infection Control

Health Promotion and Maintenance

Psychosocial Integrity

Physiological Integrity: Basic Care and Comfort, Pharmacological and Parenteral Therapies, Reduction of Risk Potential, and Physiological Adaptation

CARE ACCORDING TO QUALITY AND SAFETY STANDARDS

Patient-Centered Care

Teamwork and Collaboration

Evidence-Based Practice

Quality Improvement

Safety

Informatics

Buddy Review: _____   Faculty Review: _____

Grade Tracker

Related Exemplars

Related Concepts

Classroom Critical Thinking

Reading / Resources Critical Thinking

Priority Assessments

1
2
3

Priority Labs & Diagnostics

1
2
3

Priority Nursing Interventions

1
2
3

Priority Medications

1
2
3

Priority Potential & Actual Complications

1
2
3

Priority Collaborative Goals

1
2
3

NurseThink Quick

CARE ACCORDING TO THE NCLEX® TEST PLAN

Safe and Effective Care: Management of Care, Coordinated Care, Safety and Infection Control

Health Promotion and Maintenance

Psychosocial Integrity

Physiological Integrity: Basic Care and Comfort, Pharmacological and Parenteral Therapies, Reduction of Risk Potential, and Physiological Adaptation

CARE ACCORDING TO QUALITY AND SAFETY STANDARDS

Patient-Centered Care

Teamwork and Collaboration

Evidence-Based Practice

Quality Improvement

Safety

Informatics

Buddy Review: _____   Faculty Review: _____

Grade Tracker

Related Exemplars

Related Concepts

Classroom Critical Thinking

Reading / Resources Critical Thinking

Priority Assessments

1
2
3

Priority Labs & Diagnostics

1
2
3

Priority Nursing Interventions

1
2
3

Priority Medications

1
2
3

Priority Potential & Actual Complications

1
2
3

Priority Collaborative Goals

1
2
3

NurseThink Quick

CARE ACCORDING TO THE NCLEX® TEST PLAN

Safe and Effective Care: Management of Care, Coordinated Care, Safety and Infection Control

Health Promotion and Maintenance

Psychosocial Integrity

Physiological Integrity: Basic Care and Comfort, Pharmacological and Parenteral Therapies, Reduction of Risk Potential, and Physiological Adaptation

CARE ACCORDING TO QUALITY AND SAFETY STANDARDS

Patient-Centered Care

Teamwork and Collaboration

Evidence-Based Practice

Quality Improvement

Safety

Informatics

Buddy Review: _____   Faculty Review: _____

Grade Tracker

Related Exemplars	**Related Concepts**

Classroom Critical Thinking	**Reading / Resources Critical Thinking**

Priority Assessments

1
2
3

Priority Labs & Diagnostics

1
2
3

Priority Nursing Interventions

1
2
3

Priority Medications

1

2

3

Priority Potential & Actual Complications

1

2

3

Priority Collaborative Goals

1

2

3

NurseThink Quick

CARE ACCORDING TO THE NCLEX® TEST PLAN

Safe and Effective Care: Management of Care, Coordinated Care, Safety and Infection Control

Health Promotion and Maintenance

Psychosocial Integrity

Physiological Integrity: Basic Care and Comfort, Pharmacological and Parenteral Therapies, Reduction of Risk Potential, and Physiological Adaptation

CARE ACCORDING TO QUALITY AND SAFETY STANDARDS

Patient-Centered Care

Teamwork and Collaboration

Evidence-Based Practice

Quality Improvement

Safety

Informatics

Buddy Review: _____   Faculty Review: _____

Grade Tracker

Related Exemplars

Related Concepts

Classroom Critical Thinking

Reading / Resources Critical Thinking

Priority Assessments

1
2
3

Priority Labs & Diagnostics

1
2
3

Priority Nursing Interventions

1
2
3

Priority Medications

1
2
3

Priority Potential & Actual Complications

1
2
3

Priority Collaborative Goals

1
2
3

NurseThink Quick

CARE ACCORDING TO THE NCLEX® TEST PLAN

Safe and Effective Care: Management of Care, Coordinated Care, Safety and Infection Control

Health Promotion and Maintenance

Psychosocial Integrity

Physiological Integrity: Basic Care and Comfort, Pharmacological and Parenteral Therapies, Reduction of Risk Potential, and Physiological Adaptation

CARE ACCORDING TO QUALITY AND SAFETY STANDARDS

Patient-Centered Care

Teamwork and Collaboration

Evidence-Based Practice

Quality Improvement

Safety

Informatics

Buddy Review: _____   Faculty Review: _____

Grade Tracker

Related Exemplars

Related Concepts

Classroom Critical Thinking

Reading / Resources Critical Thinking

Priority Assessments

1
2
3

Priority Labs & Diagnostics

1
2
3

Priority Nursing Interventions

1
2
3

Priority Medications

1

2

3

Priority Potential & Actual Complications

1

2

3

Priority Collaborative Goals

1

2

3

NurseThink Quick

CARE ACCORDING TO THE NCLEX® TEST PLAN

Safe and Effective Care: Management of Care, Coordinated Care, Safety and Infection Control

Health Promotion and Maintenance

Psychosocial Integrity

Physiological Integrity: Basic Care and Comfort, Pharmacological and Parenteral Therapies, Reduction of Risk Potential, and Physiological Adaptation

CARE ACCORDING TO QUALITY AND SAFETY STANDARDS

Patient-Centered Care

Teamwork and Collaboration

Evidence-Based Practice

Quality Improvement

Safety

Informatics

Buddy Review: _____   Faculty Review: _____

Grade Tracker

Related Exemplars	**Related Concepts**

Classroom Critical Thinking	**Reading / Resources Critical Thinking**

Priority Assessments	**Priority Labs & Diagnostics**	**Priority Nursing Interventions**
1	1	1
2	2	2
3	3	3

Priority Medications	**Priority Potential & Actual Complications**	**Priority Collaborative Goals**
1	1	1
2	2	2
3	3	3

NurseThink Quick

CARE ACCORDING TO THE NCLEX® TEST PLAN

Safe and Effective Care: Management of Care, Coordinated Care, Safety and Infection Control

Health Promotion and Maintenance

Psychosocial Integrity

Physiological Integrity: Basic Care and Comfort, Pharmacological and Parenteral Therapies, Reduction of Risk Potential, and Physiological Adaptation

CARE ACCORDING TO QUALITY AND SAFETY STANDARDS

Patient-Centered Care

Teamwork and Collaboration

Evidence-Based Practice

Quality Improvement

Safety

Informatics

Buddy Review: _____   Faculty Review: _____

Grade Tracker

Nurse Think Notes

Syndrome of Inappropriate Antidiuretic Hormone

Related Exemplars	Related Concepts

Classroom Critical Thinking	Reading / Resources Critical Thinking

Priority Assessments

1
2
3

Priority Labs & Diagnostics

1
2
3

Priority Nursing Interventions

1
2
3

Priority Medications

1

2

3

Priority Potential & Actual Complications

1

2

3

Priority Collaborative Goals

1

2

3

NurseThink Quick

SIADH: Inducing Drugs	**SIADH: Causes**	
ABCD	***SIADH***	
Analgesics: opioids, NSAIDs	**S**urgery	
Barbiturates	**I**ntracranial: infection, head injury, CVA	
Cyclophosphamide/Chlorpromazine/ Carbamazepine	**A**lveolar: cancer, pus	
Diuretic (thiazide)	**D**rugs	
	Hormonal: hypothyroid, low corticosteroid level	

CARE ACCORDING TO THE NCLEX® TEST PLAN

Safe and Effective Care: Management of Care, Coordinated Care, Safety and Infection Control

Health Promotion and Maintenance

Psychosocial Integrity

Physiological Integrity: Basic Care and Comfort, Pharmacological and Parenteral Therapies, Reduction of Risk Potential, and Physiological Adaptation

CARE ACCORDING TO QUALITY AND SAFETY STANDARDS

Patient-Centered Care

Teamwork and Collaboration

Evidence-Based Practice

Quality Improvement

Safety

Informatics

Buddy Review: _____   Faculty Review: _____

Grade Tracker

Related Exemplars

Related Concepts

Classroom Critical Thinking

Reading / Resources Critical Thinking

Priority Assessments

1
2
3

Priority Labs & Diagnostics

1
2
3

Priority Nursing Interventions

1
2
3

Priority Medications

1
2
3

Priority Potential & Actual Complications

1
2
3

Priority Collaborative Goals

1
2
3

NurseThink Quick

Thyroid Storm: Initial Management	**Hyperthyroidism: Signs and Symptoms**	
PCP's **P**TU – 1gm PO **C**orticosteroids **P**ropranolol **S**SKI	***Thyroidism*** **T**remor **H**eart rate up **Y**awning (fatigability) **R**estlessness **O**ligomenorrhea & amenorrhea **I**ntolerance to heat **D**iarrhea **I**rritability **S**weating **M**uscle wasting & weight loss	

CARE ACCORDING TO THE NCLEX® TEST PLAN

Safe and Effective Care: Management of Care, Coordinated Care, Safety and Infection Control

Health Promotion and Maintenance

Psychosocial Integrity

Physiological Integrity: Basic Care and Comfort, Pharmacological and Parenteral Therapies, Reduction of Risk Potential, and Physiological Adaptation

CARE ACCORDING TO QUALITY AND SAFETY STANDARDS

Patient-Centered Care

Teamwork and Collaboration

Evidence-Based Practice

Quality Improvement

Safety

Informatics

Buddy Review: _____   Faculty Review: _____

Grade Tracker

Related Exemplars

Related Concepts

Classroom Critical Thinking

Reading / Resources Critical Thinking

Priority Assessments

1

2

3

Priority Labs & Diagnostics

1

2

3

Priority Nursing Interventions

1

2

3

Priority Medications

1

2

3

Priority Potential & Actual Complications

1

2

3

Priority Collaborative Goals

1

2

3

NurseThink Quick

CARE ACCORDING TO THE NCLEX® TEST PLAN

Safe and Effective Care: Management of Care, Coordinated Care, Safety and Infection Control

Health Promotion and Maintenance

Psychosocial Integrity

Physiological Integrity: Basic Care and Comfort, Pharmacological and Parenteral Therapies, Reduction of Risk Potential, and Physiological Adaptation

CARE ACCORDING TO QUALITY AND SAFETY STANDARDS

Patient-Centered Care

Teamwork and Collaboration

Evidence-Based Practice

Quality Improvement

Safety

Informatics

Buddy Review: _____ Faculty Review: _____

Grade Tracker

Related Exemplars	**Related Concepts**

Classroom Critical Thinking	**Reading / Resources Critical Thinking**

Priority Assessments

1

2

3

Priority Labs & Diagnostics

1

2

3

Priority Nursing Interventions

1

2

3

Priority Medications

1

2

3

Priority Potential & Actual Complications

1

2

3

Priority Collaborative Goals

1

2

3

NurseThink Quick

CARE ACCORDING TO THE NCLEX® TEST PLAN

Safe and Effective Care: Management of Care, Coordinated Care, Safety and Infection Control

Health Promotion and Maintenance

Psychosocial Integrity

Physiological Integrity: Basic Care and Comfort, Pharmacological and Parenteral Therapies, Reduction of Risk Potential, and Physiological Adaptation

CARE ACCORDING TO QUALITY AND SAFETY STANDARDS

Patient-Centered Care

Teamwork and Collaboration

Evidence-Based Practice

Quality Improvement

Safety

Informatics

Buddy Review: _____   Faculty Review: _____

Grade Tracker

Related Exemplars	**Related Concepts**

Classroom Critical Thinking	**Reading / Resources Critical Thinking**

Priority Assessments

1

2

3

Priority Labs & Diagnostics

1

2

3

Priority Nursing Interventions

1

2

3

Priority Medications

1

2

3

Priority Potential & Actual Complications

1

2

3

Priority Collaborative Goals

1

2

3

NurseThink Quick

H. Pylori Treatment	Peptic Ulcer: Associated Causes	
Please Make Tummy Better	***Shazam***	
Proton pump inhibitor	**S**moking	
Metronidazole	**H**ypercalcemia	
Tetracycline	**A**spirin	
Bismuth	**Z**ollinger-Ellison	
	Acidity	
	MEN Type 1	

CARE ACCORDING TO THE NCLEX® TEST PLAN

Safe and Effective Care: Management of Care, Coordinated Care, Safety and Infection Control

Health Promotion and Maintenance

Psychosocial Integrity

Physiological Integrity: Basic Care and Comfort, Pharmacological and Parenteral Therapies, Reduction of Risk Potential, and Physiological Adaptation

CARE ACCORDING TO QUALITY AND SAFETY STANDARDS

Patient-Centered Care

Teamwork and Collaboration

Evidence-Based Practice

Quality Improvement

Safety

Informatics

Buddy Review: _____   Faculty Review: _____

Grade Tracker

Related Exemplars

Related Concepts

Classroom Critical Thinking

Reading / Resources Critical Thinking

Priority Assessments

1

2

3

Priority Labs & Diagnostics

1

2

3

Priority Nursing Interventions

1

2

3

Priority Medications

1

2

3

Priority Potential & Actual Complications

1

2

3

Priority Collaborative Goals

1

2

3

NurseThink Quick

CARE ACCORDING TO THE NCLEX® TEST PLAN

Safe and Effective Care: Management of Care, Coordinated Care, Safety and Infection Control

Health Promotion and Maintenance

Psychosocial Integrity

Physiological Integrity: Basic Care and Comfort, Pharmacological and Parenteral Therapies, Reduction of Risk Potential, and Physiological Adaptation

CARE ACCORDING TO QUALITY AND SAFETY STANDARDS

Patient-Centered Care

Teamwork and Collaboration

Evidence-Based Practice

Quality Improvement

Safety

Informatics

Buddy Review: _____   Faculty Review: _____

Grade Tracker

Related Exemplars	**Related Concepts**

Classroom Critical Thinking	**Reading / Resources Critical Thinking**

Priority Assessments

1
2
3

Priority Labs & Diagnostics

1
2
3

Priority Nursing Interventions

1
2
3

Priority Medications

1

2

3

Priority Potential & Actual Complications

1

2

3

Priority Collaborative Goals

1

2

3

NurseThink Quick

Renal Failure: Management		
AEIOU **A**nemia/Acidosis **E**lectrolytes and fluids **I**nfections **O**ther measures (nutrition, nausea, vomiting) **U**remia		

CARE ACCORDING TO THE NCLEX® TEST PLAN

Safe and Effective Care: Management of Care, Coordinated Care, Safety and Infection Control

Health Promotion and Maintenance

Psychosocial Integrity

Physiological Integrity: Basic Care and Comfort, Pharmacological and Parenteral Therapies, Reduction of Risk Potential, and Physiological Adaptation

CARE ACCORDING TO QUALITY AND SAFETY STANDARDS

Patient-Centered Care

Teamwork and Collaboration

Evidence-Based Practice

Quality Improvement

Safety

Informatics

Buddy Review: _____   Faculty Review: _____

Grade Tracker

NurseThink Notes

Related Exemplars

Related Concepts

Classroom Critical Thinking

Reading / Resources Critical Thinking

Priority Assessments

1
2
3

Priority Labs & Diagnostics

1
2
3

Priority Nursing Interventions

1
2
3

Priority Medications

1
2
3

Priority Potential & Actual Complications

1
2
3

Priority Collaborative Goals

1
2
3

NurseThink Quick

CARE ACCORDING TO THE NCLEX® TEST PLAN

Safe and Effective Care: Management of Care, Coordinated Care, Safety and Infection Control

Health Promotion and Maintenance

Psychosocial Integrity

Physiological Integrity: Basic Care and Comfort, Pharmacological and Parenteral Therapies, Reduction of Risk Potential, and Physiological Adaptation

CARE ACCORDING TO QUALITY AND SAFETY STANDARDS

Patient-Centered Care

Teamwork and Collaboration

Evidence-Based Practice

Quality Improvement

Safety

Informatics

Buddy Review: _____   Faculty Review: _____

Grade Tracker

NurseThink Notes

Related Exemplars

Related Concepts

Classroom Critical Thinking

Reading / Resources Critical Thinking

Priority Assessments
1
2
3

Priority Labs & Diagnostics
1
2
3

Priority Nursing Interventions
1
2
3

Priority Medications
1
2
3

Priority Potential & Actual Complications
1
2
3

Priority Collaborative Goals
1
2
3

NurseThink Notes

Chronic Kidney Disease/End Stage Renal Disease

NurseThink Quick

Chronic Renal Failure: Causes	Renal Failure: Symptoms/Signs	Renal Failure: Consequences
Glad Shop	***Get Vinny Prepared, He's Not Making Big Pee***	***ABCDEFG***
Glomerulonephritis	**G**I motility	**A**nemia
Lupus	**V**omiting	**B**one alterations
Analgesics	**P**ruritus	**C**ardiopulmonary
Diabetes	**H**eadache	**V**itamin D loss
Systemic vascular disease	**N**ausea	**E**lectrolyte imbalance
Hypertension	**M**alaise	**F**everous infections
Obstruction	**B**reathlessness	**G**I disturbances
Polycystic kidney disease	**P**igmentation	

CARE ACCORDING TO THE NCLEX® TEST PLAN

Safe and Effective Care: Management of Care, Coordinated Care, Safety and Infection Control

Health Promotion and Maintenance

Psychosocial Integrity

Physiological Integrity: Basic Care and Comfort, Pharmacological and Parenteral Therapies, Reduction of Risk Potential, and Physiological Adaptation

CARE ACCORDING TO QUALITY AND SAFETY STANDARDS

Patient-Centered Care

Teamwork and Collaboration

Evidence-Based Practice

Quality Improvement

Safety

Informatics

Buddy Review: _____   Faculty Review: _____

Grade Tracker

Related Exemplars	Related Concepts

Classroom Critical Thinking	Reading / Resources Critical Thinking

Priority Assessments

1
2
3

Priority Labs & Diagnostics

1
2
3

Priority Nursing Interventions

1
2
3

Priority Medications

1

2

3

Priority Potential & Actual Complications

1

2

3

Priority Collaborative Goals

1

2

3

CARE ACCORDING TO THE NCLEX® TEST PLAN

Safe and Effective Care: Management of Care, Coordinated Care, Safety and Infection Control

Health Promotion and Maintenance

Psychosocial Integrity

Physiological Integrity: Basic Care and Comfort, Pharmacological and Parenteral Therapies, Reduction of Risk Potential, and Physiological Adaptation

CARE ACCORDING TO QUALITY AND SAFETY STANDARDS

Patient-Centered Care

Teamwork and Collaboration

Evidence-Based Practice

Quality Improvement

Safety

Informatics

Buddy Review: _____   Faculty Review: _____

Grade Tracker

Related Exemplars

Related Concepts

Classroom Critical Thinking

Reading / Resources Critical Thinking

Priority Assessments

1
2
3

Priority Labs & Diagnostics

1
2
3

Priority Nursing Interventions

1
2
3

Priority Medications

1
2
3

Priority Potential & Actual Complications

1
2
3

Priority Collaborative Goals

1
2
3

NurseThink Quick

CARE ACCORDING TO THE NCLEX® TEST PLAN

Safe and Effective Care: Management of Care, Coordinated Care, Safety and Infection Control

Health Promotion and Maintenance

Psychosocial Integrity

Physiological Integrity: Basic Care and Comfort, Pharmacological and Parenteral Therapies, Reduction of Risk Potential, and Physiological Adaptation

CARE ACCORDING TO QUALITY AND SAFETY STANDARDS

Patient-Centered Care

Teamwork and Collaboration

Evidence-Based Practice

Quality Improvement

Safety

Informatics

Buddy Review: _____   Faculty Review: _____

Grade Tracker

Related Exemplars

Related Concepts

Classroom Critical Thinking

Reading / Resources Critical Thinking

Priority Assessments

1

2

3

Priority Labs & Diagnostics

1

2

3

Priority Nursing Interventions

1

2

3

Priority Medications

1

2

3

Priority Potential & Actual Complications

1

2

3

Priority Collaborative Goals

1

2

3

NurseThink Quick

Asthma: Precipitating Factors	Asthma: Treatments
Diplomat	**Asthma**
Drugs (aspirin, NSAIDs, Beta blockers)	**A**drenergics
Infections	**S**teroids
Pollutants (home, work)	**T**heophyllines
Laughter (emotion)	**H**ydration
O – Esophageal Reflux (nocturnal asthma)	**M**ask O2
Mites	**A**BGs
Activity and Exercise	
Temperature (cold)	

CARE ACCORDING TO THE NCLEX® TEST PLAN

Safe and Effective Care: Management of Care, Coordinated Care, Safety and Infection Control

Health Promotion and Maintenance

Psychosocial Integrity

Physiological Integrity: Basic Care and Comfort, Pharmacological and Parenteral Therapies, Reduction of Risk Potential, and Physiological Adaptation

CARE ACCORDING TO QUALITY AND SAFETY STANDARDS

Patient-Centered Care

Teamwork and Collaboration

Evidence-Based Practice

Quality Improvement

Safety

Informatics

Buddy Review: _____   Faculty Review: _____

Grade Tracker

Related Exemplars

Related Concepts

Classroom Critical Thinking

Reading / Resources Critical Thinking

Priority Assessments

1
2
3

Priority Labs & Diagnostics

1
2
3

Priority Nursing Interventions

1
2
3

Priority Medications

1
2
3

Priority Potential & Actual Complications

1
2
3

Priority Collaborative Goals

1
2
3

NurseThink Quick

COPD:	**COPD: 4 Types**	**Emphysema**
Emphysema has the letter P = Pink puffer Bronchitis has the letter B = Blue bloater	***ABCDE*** **A**sthma **B**ronchiectasis **C**hronic bronchitis **D**yspnea **E**mphysema	***Cigarettes Is Primary Problem*** **C**igarettes **I**nflammation healed to scar **P**rotease inhibitor deficiency **P**neumothorax

CARE ACCORDING TO THE NCLEX® TEST PLAN

Safe and Effective Care: Management of Care, Coordinated Care, Safety and Infection Control

Health Promotion and Maintenance

Psychosocial Integrity

Physiological Integrity: Basic Care and Comfort, Pharmacological and Parenteral Therapies, Reduction of Risk Potential, and Physiological Adaptation

CARE ACCORDING TO QUALITY AND SAFETY STANDARDS

Patient-Centered Care

Teamwork and Collaboration

Evidence-Based Practice

Quality Improvement

Safety

Informatics

Buddy Review: _____   Faculty Review: _____

Grade Tracker

Related Exemplars	Related Concepts

Classroom Critical Thinking	Reading / Resources Critical Thinking

Priority Assessments

1

2

3

Priority Labs & Diagnostics

1

2

3

Priority Nursing Interventions

1

2

3

Priority Medications

1

2

3

Priority Potential & Actual Complications

1

2

3

Priority Collaborative Goals

1

2

3

NurseThink Quick

CARE ACCORDING TO THE NCLEX® TEST PLAN

Safe and Effective Care: Management of Care, Coordinated Care, Safety and Infection Control

Health Promotion and Maintenance

Psychosocial Integrity

Physiological Integrity: Basic Care and Comfort, Pharmacological and Parenteral Therapies, Reduction of Risk Potential, and Physiological Adaptation

CARE ACCORDING TO QUALITY AND SAFETY STANDARDS

Patient-Centered Care

Teamwork and Collaboration

Evidence-Based Practice

Quality Improvement

Safety

Informatics

Buddy Review: _____   Faculty Review: _____

Grade Tracker

Related Exemplars

Related Concepts

Classroom Critical Thinking

Reading / Resources Critical Thinking

Priority Assessments

1
2
3

Priority Labs & Diagnostics

1
2
3

Priority Nursing Interventions

1
2
3

Priority Medications

1
2
3

Priority Potential & Actual Complications

1
2
3

Priority Collaborative Goals

1
2
3

NurseThink Quick

CARE ACCORDING TO THE NCLEX® TEST PLAN

Safe and Effective Care: Management of Care, Coordinated Care, Safety and Infection Control

Health Promotion and Maintenance

Psychosocial Integrity

Physiological Integrity: Basic Care and Comfort, Pharmacological and Parenteral Therapies, Reduction of Risk Potential, and Physiological Adaptation

CARE ACCORDING TO QUALITY AND SAFETY STANDARDS

Patient-Centered Care

Teamwork and Collaboration

Evidence-Based Practice

Quality Improvement

Safety

Informatics

Buddy Review: _____   Faculty Review: _____

Grade Tracker

Related Exemplars

Related Concepts

Classroom Critical Thinking

Reading / Resources Critical Thinking

Priority Assessments

1

2

3

Priority Labs & Diagnostics

1

2

3

Priority Nursing Interventions

1

2

3

Priority Medications

1

2

3

Priority Potential & Actual Complications

1

2

3

Priority Collaborative Goals

1

2

3

NurseThink Quick

Acute Respiratory Failure: Type II (Hypoventilation) Criteria	Ventilator Settings: Difference between A/C and SIMV Ventilation	ARDS Causes

Acute Respiratory Failure: Type II (Hypoventilation) Criteria
50/50 Rule
PaCO2 >50
PaO2 <50 (on >50% oxygen)

Respiratory Depression Drugs
Stop
Sedatives and hypnotics
Trimethoprim
Opiates
Polymyxins

Ventilator Settings: Difference between A/C and SIMV Ventilation
A/C - Always assists (patient effort triggers vent breath delivery!)
SIMV - Sometimes assists

ARDS Causes
AAAARDDDDDSSS
Aspiration
Acute pancreatitis
Air embolism
Amniotic embolism
Radiation
DIC
Drugs
Dialysis
Drowning
Diffuse lung infection
Shock
Sepsis
Smoke inhalation

CARE ACCORDING TO THE NCLEX® TEST PLAN

Safe and Effective Care: Management of Care, Coordinated Care, Safety and Infection Control

Health Promotion and Maintenance

Psychosocial Integrity

Physiological Integrity: Basic Care and Comfort, Pharmacological and Parenteral Therapies, Reduction of Risk Potential, and Physiological Adaptation

CARE ACCORDING TO QUALITY AND SAFETY STANDARDS

Patient-Centered Care

Teamwork and Collaboration

Evidence-Based Practice

Quality Improvement

Safety

Informatics

Buddy Review: _____   Faculty Review: _____

Grade Tracker

Related Exemplars

Related Concepts

Classroom Critical Thinking

Reading / Resources Critical Thinking

Priority Assessments

1
2
3

Priority Labs & Diagnostics

1
2
3

Priority Nursing Interventions

1
2
3

Priority Medications

1
2
3

Priority Potential & Actual Complications

1
2
3

Priority Collaborative Goals

1
2
3

NurseThink Quick

CARE ACCORDING TO THE NCLEX® TEST PLAN

Safe and Effective Care: Management of Care, Coordinated Care, Safety and Infection Control

Health Promotion and Maintenance

Psychosocial Integrity

Physiological Integrity: Basic Care and Comfort, Pharmacological and Parenteral Therapies, Reduction of Risk Potential, and Physiological Adaptation

CARE ACCORDING TO QUALITY AND SAFETY STANDARDS

Patient-Centered Care

Teamwork and Collaboration

Evidence-Based Practice

Quality Improvement

Safety

Informatics

Buddy Review: _____   Faculty Review: _____

Grade Tracker

Related Exemplars	Related Concepts

Classroom Critical Thinking	Reading / Resources Critical Thinking

Priority Assessments

1
2
3

Priority Labs & Diagnostics

1
2
3

Priority Nursing Interventions

1
2
3

Priority Medications

1
2
3

Priority Potential & Actual Complications

1
2
3

Priority Collaborative Goals

1
2
3

NurseThink Quick

CARE ACCORDING TO THE NCLEX® TEST PLAN

Safe and Effective Care: Management of Care, Coordinated Care, Safety and Infection Control

Health Promotion and Maintenance

Psychosocial Integrity

Physiological Integrity: Basic Care and Comfort, Pharmacological and Parenteral Therapies, Reduction of Risk Potential, and Physiological Adaptation

CARE ACCORDING TO QUALITY AND SAFETY STANDARDS

Patient-Centered Care

Teamwork and Collaboration

Evidence-Based Practice

Quality Improvement

Safety

Informatics

Buddy Review: _____   Faculty Review: _____

Grade Tracker

Related Exemplars	**Related Concepts**

Classroom Critical Thinking	**Reading / Resources Critical Thinking**

Priority Assessments	**Priority Labs & Diagnostics**	**Priority Nursing Interventions**
1	1	1
2	2	2
3	3	3

Priority Medications	**Priority Potential & Actual Complications**	**Priority Collaborative Goals**
1	1	1
2	2	2
3	3	3

NurseThink Quick

CARE ACCORDING TO THE NCLEX® TEST PLAN

Safe and Effective Care: Management of Care, Coordinated Care, Safety and Infection Control

Health Promotion and Maintenance

Psychosocial Integrity

Physiological Integrity: Basic Care and Comfort, Pharmacological and Parenteral Therapies, Reduction of Risk Potential, and Physiological Adaptation

CARE ACCORDING TO QUALITY AND SAFETY STANDARDS

Patient-Centered Care

Teamwork and Collaboration

Evidence-Based Practice

Quality Improvement

Safety

Informatics

Buddy Review: _____   Faculty Review: _____

Grade Tracker

Related Exemplars

Related Concepts

Classroom Critical Thinking

Reading / Resources Critical Thinking

Priority Assessments

1
2
3

Priority Labs & Diagnostics

1
2
3

Priority Nursing Interventions

1
2
3

Priority Medications

1

2

3

Priority Potential & Actual Complications

1

2

3

Priority Collaborative Goals

1

2

3

NurseThink Quick

CARE ACCORDING TO THE NCLEX® TEST PLAN

Safe and Effective Care: Management of Care, Coordinated Care, Safety and Infection Control

Health Promotion and Maintenance

Psychosocial Integrity

Physiological Integrity: Basic Care and Comfort, Pharmacological and Parenteral Therapies, Reduction of Risk Potential, and Physiological Adaptation

CARE ACCORDING TO QUALITY AND SAFETY STANDARDS

Patient-Centered Care

Teamwork and Collaboration

Evidence-Based Practice

Quality Improvement

Safety

Informatics

Buddy Review: _____   Faculty Review: _____

Grade Tracker

Related Exemplars

Related Concepts

Classroom Critical Thinking

Reading / Resources Critical Thinking

Priority Assessments

1

2

3

Priority Labs & Diagnostics

1

2

3

Priority Nursing Interventions

1

2

3

Priority Medications

1

2

3

Priority Potential & Actual Complications

1

2

3

Priority Collaborative Goals

1

2

3

NurseThink Quick

CARE ACCORDING TO THE NCLEX® TEST PLAN

Safe and Effective Care: Management of Care, Coordinated Care, Safety and Infection Control

Health Promotion and Maintenance

Psychosocial Integrity

Physiological Integrity: Basic Care and Comfort, Pharmacological and Parenteral Therapies, Reduction of Risk Potential, and Physiological Adaptation

CARE ACCORDING TO QUALITY AND SAFETY STANDARDS

Patient-Centered Care

Teamwork and Collaboration

Evidence-Based Practice

Quality Improvement

Safety

Informatics

Buddy Review: _____   Faculty Review: _____

Grade Tracker

Related Exemplars

Related Concepts

Classroom Critical Thinking

Reading / Resources Critical Thinking

Priority Assessments

1
2
3

Priority Labs & Diagnostics

1
2
3

Priority Nursing Interventions

1
2
3

Priority Medications

1
2
3

Priority Potential & Actual Complications

1
2
3

Priority Collaborative Goals

1
2
3

NurseThink Quick

CARE ACCORDING TO THE NCLEX® TEST PLAN

Safe and Effective Care: Management of Care, Coordinated Care, Safety and Infection Control

Health Promotion and Maintenance

Psychosocial Integrity

Physiological Integrity: Basic Care and Comfort, Pharmacological and Parenteral Therapies, Reduction of Risk Potential, and Physiological Adaptation

CARE ACCORDING TO QUALITY AND SAFETY STANDARDS

Patient-Centered Care

Teamwork and Collaboration

Evidence-Based Practice

Quality Improvement

Safety

Informatics

Buddy Review: _____   Faculty Review: _____

Grade Tracker

Related Exemplars

Related Concepts

Classroom Critical Thinking

Reading / Resources Critical Thinking

Priority Assessments

1
2
3

Priority Labs & Diagnostics

1
2
3

Priority Nursing Interventions

1
2
3

Priority Medications

1
2
3

Priority Potential & Actual Complications

1
2
3

Priority Collaborative Goals

1
2
3

NurseThink Quick

CARE ACCORDING TO THE NCLEX® TEST PLAN

Safe and Effective Care: Management of Care, Coordinated Care, Safety and Infection Control

Health Promotion and Maintenance

Psychosocial Integrity

Physiological Integrity: Basic Care and Comfort, Pharmacological and Parenteral Therapies, Reduction of Risk Potential, and Physiological Adaptation

CARE ACCORDING TO QUALITY AND SAFETY STANDARDS

Patient-Centered Care

Teamwork and Collaboration

Evidence-Based Practice

Quality Improvement

Safety

Informatics

Buddy Review: _____   Faculty Review: _____

Grade Tracker

Related Exemplars	Related Concepts

Classroom Critical Thinking	Reading / Resources Critical Thinking

Priority Assessments

1

2

3

Priority Labs & Diagnostics

1

2

3

Priority Nursing Interventions

1

2

3

Priority Medications

1

2

3

Priority Potential & Actual Complications

1

2

3

Priority Collaborative Goals

1

2

3

CARE ACCORDING TO THE NCLEX® TEST PLAN

Safe and Effective Care: Management of Care, Coordinated Care, Safety and Infection Control

Health Promotion and Maintenance

Psychosocial Integrity

Physiological Integrity: Basic Care and Comfort, Pharmacological and Parenteral Therapies, Reduction of Risk Potential, and Physiological Adaptation

CARE ACCORDING TO QUALITY AND SAFETY STANDARDS

Patient-Centered Care

Teamwork and Collaboration

Evidence-Based Practice

Quality Improvement

Safety

Informatics

Buddy Review: _____   Faculty Review: _____

Grade Tracker

Related Exemplars	Related Concepts

Classroom Critical Thinking	Reading / Resources Critical Thinking

Priority Assessments

1
2
3

Priority Labs & Diagnostics

1
2
3

Priority Nursing Interventions

1
2
3

Priority Medications

1

2

3

Priority Potential & Actual Complications

1

2

3

Priority Collaborative Goals

1

2

3

NurseThink Quick

CARE ACCORDING TO THE NCLEX® TEST PLAN

Safe and Effective Care: Management of Care, Coordinated Care, Safety and Infection Control

Health Promotion and Maintenance

Psychosocial Integrity

Physiological Integrity: Basic Care and Comfort, Pharmacological and Parenteral Therapies, Reduction of Risk Potential, and Physiological Adaptation

CARE ACCORDING TO QUALITY AND SAFETY STANDARDS

Patient-Centered Care

Teamwork and Collaboration

Evidence-Based Practice

Quality Improvement

Safety

Informatics

Buddy Review: _____   Faculty Review: _____

Grade Tracker

Related Exemplars

Related Concepts

Classroom Critical Thinking

Reading / Resources Critical Thinking

Priority Assessments

1

2

3

Priority Labs & Diagnostics

1

2

3

Priority Nursing Interventions

1

2

3

Priority Medications

1

2

3

Priority Potential & Actual Complications

1

2

3

Priority Collaborative Goals

1

2

3

NurseThink Notes

NurseThink Quick

CARE ACCORDING TO THE NCLEX® TEST PLAN

Safe and Effective Care: Management of Care, Coordinated Care, Safety and Infection Control

Health Promotion and Maintenance

Psychosocial Integrity

Physiological Integrity: Basic Care and Comfort, Pharmacological and Parenteral Therapies, Reduction of Risk Potential, and Physiological Adaptation

CARE ACCORDING TO QUALITY AND SAFETY STANDARDS

Patient-Centered Care

Teamwork and Collaboration

Evidence-Based Practice

Quality Improvement

Safety

Informatics

Buddy Review: _____   Faculty Review: _____

Grade Tracker

Related Exemplars	Related Concepts

Classroom Critical Thinking	Reading / Resources Critical Thinking

Priority Assessments

1
2
3

Priority Labs & Diagnostics

1
2
3

Priority Nursing Interventions

1
2
3

Priority Medications

1
2
3

Priority Potential & Actual Complications

1
2
3

Priority Collaborative Goals

1
2
3

NurseThink Quick

CARE ACCORDING TO THE NCLEX® TEST PLAN

Safe and Effective Care: Management of Care, Coordinated Care, Safety and Infection Control

Health Promotion and Maintenance

Psychosocial Integrity

Physiological Integrity: Basic Care and Comfort, Pharmacological and Parenteral Therapies, Reduction of Risk Potential, and Physiological Adaptation

CARE ACCORDING TO QUALITY AND SAFETY STANDARDS

Patient-Centered Care

Teamwork and Collaboration

Evidence-Based Practice

Quality Improvement

Safety

Informatics

Buddy Review: _____   Faculty Review: _____

Grade Tracker

Related Exemplars	Related Concepts

Classroom Critical Thinking	Reading / Resources Critical Thinking

Priority Assessments

1
2
3

Priority Labs & Diagnostics

1
2
3

Priority Nursing Interventions

1
2
3

Priority Medications

1
2
3

Priority Potential & Actual Complications

1
2
3

Priority Collaborative Goals

1
2
3

NurseThink Notes

NurseThink Quick

CARE ACCORDING TO THE NCLEX® TEST PLAN

Safe and Effective Care: Management of Care, Coordinated Care, Safety and Infection Control

Health Promotion and Maintenance

Psychosocial Integrity

Physiological Integrity: Basic Care and Comfort, Pharmacological and Parenteral Therapies, Reduction of Risk Potential, and Physiological Adaptation

CARE ACCORDING TO QUALITY AND SAFETY STANDARDS

Patient-Centered Care

Teamwork and Collaboration

Evidence-Based Practice

Quality Improvement

Safety

Informatics

Buddy Review: _____   Faculty Review: _____

Grade Tracker

Related Exemplars

Related Concepts

Classroom Critical Thinking

Reading / Resources Critical Thinking

Priority Assessments

1

2

3

Priority Labs & Diagnostics

1

2

3

Priority Nursing Interventions

1

2

3

Priority Medications

1

2

3

Priority Potential & Actual Complications

1

2

3

Priority Collaborative Goals

1

2

3

NurseThink Quick

CARE ACCORDING TO THE NCLEX® TEST PLAN

Safe and Effective Care: Management of Care, Coordinated Care, Safety and Infection Control

Health Promotion and Maintenance

Psychosocial Integrity

Physiological Integrity: Basic Care and Comfort, Pharmacological and Parenteral Therapies, Reduction of Risk Potential, and Physiological Adaptation

CARE ACCORDING TO QUALITY AND SAFETY STANDARDS

Patient-Centered Care

Teamwork and Collaboration

Evidence-Based Practice

Quality Improvement

Safety

Informatics

Buddy Review: _____   Faculty Review: _____

Grade Tracker

Related Exemplars	Related Concepts

Classroom Critical Thinking	Reading / Resources Critical Thinking

Priority Assessments

1
2
3

Priority Labs & Diagnostics

1
2
3

Priority Nursing Interventions

1
2
3

Priority Medications

1

2

3

Priority Potential & Actual Complications

1

2

3

Priority Collaborative Goals

1

2

3

NurseThink Quick

CARE ACCORDING TO THE NCLEX® TEST PLAN

Safe and Effective Care: Management of Care, Coordinated Care, Safety and Infection Control

Health Promotion and Maintenance

Psychosocial Integrity

Physiological Integrity: Basic Care and Comfort, Pharmacological and Parenteral Therapies, Reduction of Risk Potential, and Physiological Adaptation

CARE ACCORDING TO QUALITY AND SAFETY STANDARDS

Patient-Centered Care

Teamwork and Collaboration

Evidence-Based Practice

Quality Improvement

Safety

Informatics

Buddy Review: _____   Faculty Review: _____

Grade Tracker

Related Exemplars	Related Concepts

Classroom Critical Thinking	Reading / Resources Critical Thinking

Priority Assessments	Priority Labs & Diagnostics	Priority Nursing Interventions
1	1	1
2	2	2
3	3	3

Priority Medications	Priority Potential & Actual Complications	Priority Collaborative Goals
1	1	1
2	2	2
3	3	3

NurseThink Quick

CARE ACCORDING TO THE NCLEX® TEST PLAN

Safe and Effective Care: Management of Care, Coordinated Care, Safety and Infection Control

Health Promotion and Maintenance

Psychosocial Integrity

Physiological Integrity: Basic Care and Comfort, Pharmacological and Parenteral Therapies, Reduction of Risk Potential, and Physiological Adaptation

CARE ACCORDING TO QUALITY AND SAFETY STANDARDS

Patient-Centered Care

Teamwork and Collaboration

Evidence-Based Practice

Quality Improvement

Safety

Informatics

Buddy Review: _____   Faculty Review: _____

Grade Tracker

Related Exemplars

Related Concepts

Classroom Critical Thinking

Reading / Resources Critical Thinking

Priority Assessments

1

2

3

Priority Labs & Diagnostics

1

2

3

Priority Nursing Interventions

1

2

3

Priority Medications

1

2

3

Priority Potential & Actual Complications

1

2

3

Priority Collaborative Goals

1

2

3

NurseThink Quick

CARE ACCORDING TO THE NCLEX® TEST PLAN

Safe and Effective Care: Management of Care, Coordinated Care, Safety and Infection Control

Health Promotion and Maintenance

Psychosocial Integrity

Physiological Integrity: Basic Care and Comfort, Pharmacological and Parenteral Therapies, Reduction of Risk Potential, and Physiological Adaptation

CARE ACCORDING TO QUALITY AND SAFETY STANDARDS

Patient-Centered Care

Teamwork and Collaboration

Evidence-Based Practice

Quality Improvement

Safety

Informatics

Buddy Review: _____   Faculty Review: _____

Grade Tracker

Related Exemplars	**Related Concepts**

Classroom Critical Thinking	**Reading / Resources Critical Thinking**

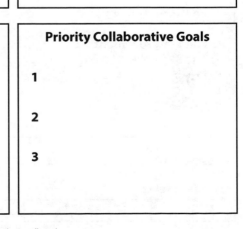

Priority Assessments

1

2

3

Priority Labs & Diagnostics

1

2

3

Priority Nursing Interventions

1

2

3

Priority Medications

1

2

3

Priority Potential & Actual Complications

1

2

3

Priority Collaborative Goals

1

2

3

NurseThink Quick

CARE ACCORDING TO THE NCLEX® TEST PLAN

Safe and Effective Care: Management of Care, Coordinated Care, Safety and Infection Control

Health Promotion and Maintenance

Psychosocial Integrity

Physiological Integrity: Basic Care and Comfort, Pharmacological and Parenteral Therapies, Reduction of Risk Potential, and Physiological Adaptation

CARE ACCORDING TO QUALITY AND SAFETY STANDARDS

Patient-Centered Care

Teamwork and Collaboration

Evidence-Based Practice

Quality Improvement

Safety

Informatics

Buddy Review: _____   Faculty Review: _____

Grade Tracker

Related Exemplars	Related Concepts

Classroom Critical Thinking	Reading / Resources Critical Thinking

Priority Assessments

1

2

3

Priority Labs & Diagnostics

1

2

3

Priority Nursing Interventions

1

2

3

Priority Medications

1

2

3

Priority Potential & Actual Complications

1

2

3

Priority Collaborative Goals

1

2

3

NurseThink Quick

CARE ACCORDING TO THE NCLEX® TEST PLAN

Safe and Effective Care: Management of Care, Coordinated Care, Safety and Infection Control

Health Promotion and Maintenance

Psychosocial Integrity

Physiological Integrity: Basic Care and Comfort, Pharmacological and Parenteral Therapies, Reduction of Risk Potential, and Physiological Adaptation

CARE ACCORDING TO QUALITY AND SAFETY STANDARDS

Patient-Centered Care

Teamwork and Collaboration

Evidence-Based Practice

Quality Improvement

Safety

Informatics

Buddy Review: _____   Faculty Review: _____

Grade Tracker

Related Exemplars

Related Concepts

Classroom Critical Thinking

Reading / Resources Critical Thinking

Priority Assessments

1

2

3

Priority Labs & Diagnostics

1

2

3

Priority Nursing Interventions

1

2

3

Priority Medications

1

2

3

Priority Potential & Actual Complications

1

2

3

Priority Collaborative Goals

1

2

3

NurseThink Quick

CARE ACCORDING TO THE NCLEX® TEST PLAN

Safe and Effective Care: Management of Care, Coordinated Care, Safety and Infection Control

Health Promotion and Maintenance

Psychosocial Integrity

Physiological Integrity: Basic Care and Comfort, Pharmacological and Parenteral Therapies, Reduction of Risk Potential, and Physiological Adaptation

CARE ACCORDING TO QUALITY AND SAFETY STANDARDS

Patient-Centered Care

Teamwork and Collaboration

Evidence-Based Practice

Quality Improvement

Safety

Informatics

Buddy Review: _____   Faculty Review: _____

Grade Tracker

Notes

_____

Related Exemplars	Related Concepts

Classroom Critical Thinking	Reading / Resources Critical Thinking

Priority Assessments
1
2
3

Priority Labs & Diagnostics
1
2
3

Priority Nursing Interventions
1
2
3

Priority Medications
1
2
3

Priority Potential & Actual Complications
1
2
3

Priority Collaborative Goals
1
2
3

CARE ACCORDING TO THE NCLEX® TEST PLAN

Safe and Effective Care: Management of Care, Coordinated Care, Safety and Infection Control

Health Promotion and Maintenance

Psychosocial Integrity

Physiological Integrity: Basic Care and Comfort, Pharmacological and Parenteral Therapies, Reduction of Risk Potential, and Physiological Adaptation

CARE ACCORDING TO QUALITY AND SAFETY STANDARDS

Patient-Centered Care

Teamwork and Collaboration

Evidence-Based Practice

Quality Improvement

Safety

Informatics

Buddy Review: _____   Faculty Review: _____

Grade Tracker

NurseThink Notes

Related Exemplars	Related Concepts

Classroom Critical Thinking	Reading / Resources Critical Thinking

Priority Assessments

1

2

3

Priority Labs & Diagnostics

1

2

3

Priority Nursing Interventions

1

2

3

Priority Medications

1

2

3

Priority Potential & Actual Complications

1

2

3

Priority Collaborative Goals

1

2

3

CARE ACCORDING TO THE NCLEX® TEST PLAN

Safe and Effective Care: Management of Care, Coordinated Care, Safety and Infection Control

Health Promotion and Maintenance

Psychosocial Integrity

Physiological Integrity: Basic Care and Comfort, Pharmacological and Parenteral Therapies, Reduction of Risk Potential, and Physiological Adaptation

CARE ACCORDING TO QUALITY AND SAFETY STANDARDS

Patient-Centered Care

Teamwork and Collaboration

Evidence-Based Practice

Quality Improvement

Safety

Informatics

Buddy Review: _____   Faculty Review: _____

Grade Tracker

NurseThink Notes

Related Exemplars	Related Concepts

Classroom Critical Thinking	Reading / Resources Critical Thinking

Priority Assessments	Priority Labs & Diagnostics	Priority Nursing Interventions
1	1	1
2	2	2
3	3	3

Priority Medications	Priority Potential & Actual Complications	Priority Collaborative Goals
1	1	1
2	2	2
3	3	3

NurseThink Quick

<table>
<tr><td></td><td></td><td></td></tr>
</table>

CARE ACCORDING TO THE NCLEX® TEST PLAN

Safe and Effective Care: Management of Care, Coordinated Care, Safety and Infection Control

Health Promotion and Maintenance

Psychosocial Integrity

Physiological Integrity: Basic Care and Comfort, Pharmacological and Parenteral Therapies, Reduction of Risk Potential, and Physiological Adaptation

CARE ACCORDING TO QUALITY AND SAFETY STANDARDS

Patient-Centered Care

Teamwork and Collaboration

Evidence-Based Practice

Quality Improvement

Safety

Informatics

Buddy Review: _____   Faculty Review: _____

Grade Tracker

<table>
<tr><td></td><td></td><td></td><td></td><td></td><td></td><td></td><td></td><td></td><td></td><td></td><td></td><td></td><td></td><td></td><td></td><td></td></tr>
</table>

_____

Related Exemplars	**Related Concepts**

Classroom Critical Thinking

Reading / Resources Critical Thinking

Priority Assessments

1
2
3

Priority Labs & Diagnostics

1
2
3

Priority Nursing Interventions

1
2
3

Priority Medications

1

2

3

Priority Potential & Actual Complications

1

2

3

Priority Collaborative Goals

1

2

3

NurseThink Quick

CARE ACCORDING TO THE NCLEX® TEST PLAN

Safe and Effective Care: Management of Care, Coordinated Care, Safety and Infection Control

Health Promotion and Maintenance

Psychosocial Integrity

Physiological Integrity: Basic Care and Comfort, Pharmacological and Parenteral Therapies, Reduction of Risk Potential, and Physiological Adaptation

CARE ACCORDING TO QUALITY AND SAFETY STANDARDS

Patient-Centered Care

Teamwork and Collaboration

Evidence-Based Practice

Quality Improvement

Safety

Informatics

Buddy Review: _____   Faculty Review: _____

Grade Tracker

 **Notes**

_____

Related Exemplars	Related Concepts

Classroom Critical Thinking

Reading / Resources Critical Thinking

Priority Assessments

1
2
3

Priority Labs & Diagnostics

1
2
3

Priority Nursing Interventions

1
2
3

Priority Medications

1

2

3

Priority Potential & Actual Complications

1

2

3

Priority Collaborative Goals

1

2

3

CARE ACCORDING TO THE NCLEX® TEST PLAN

Safe and Effective Care: Management of Care, Coordinated Care, Safety and Infection Control

Health Promotion and Maintenance

Psychosocial Integrity

Physiological Integrity: Basic Care and Comfort, Pharmacological and Parenteral Therapies, Reduction of Risk Potential, and Physiological Adaptation

CARE ACCORDING TO QUALITY AND SAFETY STANDARDS

Patient-Centered Care

Teamwork and Collaboration

Evidence-Based Practice

Quality Improvement

Safety

Informatics

Buddy Review: _____   Faculty Review: _____

Grade Tracker

 **Notes**

_____

Related Exemplars	**Related Concepts**

Classroom Critical Thinking	**Reading / Resources Critical Thinking**

Priority Assessments

1
2
3

Priority Labs & Diagnostics

1
2
3

Priority Nursing Interventions

1
2
3

Priority Medications

1

2

3

Priority Potential & Actual Complications

1

2

3

Priority Collaborative Goals

1

2

3

CARE ACCORDING TO THE NCLEX® TEST PLAN

Safe and Effective Care: Management of Care, Coordinated Care, Safety and Infection Control

Health Promotion and Maintenance

Psychosocial Integrity

Physiological Integrity: Basic Care and Comfort, Pharmacological and Parenteral Therapies, Reduction of Risk Potential, and Physiological Adaptation

CARE ACCORDING TO QUALITY AND SAFETY STANDARDS

Patient-Centered Care

Teamwork and Collaboration

Evidence-Based Practice

Quality Improvement

Safety

Informatics

Buddy Review: _____   Faculty Review: _____

Grade Tracker
